S0-CFA-071

DISCOVERING
CHANT

OXFORD COBBLESTONES.

PHOTO: JAMES JORDAN.

Other Books by
James Jordan and James Whitbourn

THE MUSICIAN'S TRUST

(G-8388)

Selected other Books on Related Topics to this Book
by James Jordan

THE MUSICIAN'S SOUL

(G-5095)

THE MUSICIAN'S SPIRIT

(G-5866)

THE MUSICIAN'S WALK

(G-6734)

TOWARDS CENTER: THE ART OF BEING FOR MUSICIANS, ACTORS, DANCERS AND TEACHERS

(G-7661)

THE MUSICIAN'S BREATH

(G-7955)

EVOIKING SOUND: SECOND EDITION WITH DVD

(G-7359)

LIGHTING A CANDLE: THE WISDOM OF ELAINE BROWN

(G-8606)

COMPANION RESOURCE:

LAUDATE
A COLLECTION OF CHANTS

SELECTED AND EDITED BY JAMES WHITBOURN
WITH A COMMENTARY FOR PERFORMERS BY ISABELLA BURNS

DISCOVERING
CHANT

Teaching Musicianship and Human Sensibilities through Chant

JAMES JORDAN

AND

JAMES WHITBOURN

with

DOMINIC GREGORIO • STEVEN PILKINGTON

AND **ISABELLA BURNS**

GIA Publications, Inc.
Chicago, IL

Discovering Chant
Teaching Musicianship and Human Sensibilities through Chant
James Jordan
James Whitbourn

Art direction/design: Martha Chlipala
Cover photo: James Jordan, Cloister at St Stephen's House,
University of Oxford, Home of Westminster Choir
College Choral Institute at Oxford

G-8812
ISBN: 978-1-62277-107-3

Copyright © 2014 GIA Publications, Inc.
7404 S. Mason Ave
Chicago IL 60638

GIA Publications, Inc.
www.giamusic.com

All rights reserved
Printed in the United States of America

Dedication to
THE WESTMINSTER
WILLIAMSON VOICES
and
THE CHORAL MUSIC
INSTITUTE AT OXFORD
ST STEPHEN'S HOUSE
OXFORD UNIVERSITY
and
To the memory and life of
Paul Salamunovich
(1927-2014)

PHOTO: JAMES JORDAN.

ARCHWAY INTO CHAPEL AT ST STEPHEN'S HOUSE, OXFORD.

TABLE OF CONTENTS

PART I

PART II

PRACTICAL APPLICATION: PLAINCHANT MATERIALS
James Whitbourn with Isabella Burns

ENTERING IN

History does not repeat itself, but patterns of historical constellations recur. (p. xi)

—Edward Lowinsky
in *Tonality and Atonality*
in *Sixteenth Century Music*

The primary purpose of prayer is not to make requests. The primary purpose is to praise, to sing, to chant. Because the essence of prayer is a song, and man cannot live without a song.

Prayer may not save us. But prayer may make us worthy of being saved. (p. 397)

—Abraham Joshua Heschel
in *Moral Grandeur and Spiritual Audacity:*
Essays

O ver the years, I have been a part of, and have witnessed firsthand, some tremendous pedagogical innovations involving music teaching and learning, and choral pedagogy. Whether it was Frauke Haasemann and her passion for Group Vocal Technique, or Edwin Gordon and Music Learning Theory, or Gail Poch explaining why he thought the Effort/Shape of Laban would open the door to a new conducting pedagogy, all shifted the stream of the way of doing things. All of these people had a common thread about what they were pursuing. All involved a risk. A risk of thinking a bit outside the box. A risk of revisiting something that was already being "taught." A risk of looking at the pedagogical challenge from another angle. And a risk to teach in a different way than you were taught. In each case, it has been my experience that the risk was well worth taking, although at the time it made those of us who were "successful" fearful and skeptical that there might just be a better way of doing things. "If it ain't broke, don't fix it"—this philosophy has kept many from discovering a better way of doing things.

I often use the expression I heard first quoted by my colleague and friend Eugene Corporon: "If you do what you always do, you are going to get what you always got." For me, that is the challenge of being a teacher. It is easy to teach the way you were taught. Old systems, techniques that masquerade as a method, and familiar ways of doing things are educational "comfort food." But I must confess that when I see or experience something that better connects the pedagogical dots, I want to not only understand those ideas but also share them with others.

TRANSFIGURATIVE TEACHING AND LEARNING THROUGH CHANT

Teaching pedagogies require us to do what we do more efficiently. To accomplish this, we must have clarity about how we really learn music. Pedagogy also requires us to make good decisions to sharpen outreach and, subsequently, our students' learning and experience. For me, this exploration into chant has transfigured the way I not only teach my choirs, but also the way I look at a score and hear its musical implications. To say that the influence of chant is everywhere is not an understatement to me these days. For the thousands of us who hold degrees in choral conducting or who have studied it, to not have been deeply exposed to chant is simply wrong. This book is a small attempt to right that wrong and point us in a very different direction.

Understanding what makes us musical is complex. But if we want our students to be aurally literate and spiritually expressive, we must be able to strip unnecessary things away so the essences of what we do can be heard *and* deeply experienced, no matter the ability of the choir. Chant allows us to see the eco-structure of music—its architectural and expressive construction. It allows us to understand how sound moves forward and carries human spirit through a community of listening and aware beings. It is no understatement to say that if we truly study chant and our ensembles are allowed to experience and discover it with conductor as explorer, it will not only open and clarify the pedagogical path for our choirs, but it will also provide transformative musical experiences for all who take the journey.

Transfiguration is a powerful word in the English language. Its use in this context implies and demands that we as musicians "re-arrange" how we listen to others, how we immerse ourselves in the sound world around us, and how we should shed previously acquired biases, and recognize the inherent simplicity in what heretofore we labeled as complex. Breath, forward movement of sound, and the community of musicians attempting to be expressive together could define what chant does. Chant can transfigure our relationship to sound and, most importantly, our relationship to others. Ascent and descent of sound is understood and experienced in a "new" way. Musicians (our students) are empowered. Conductors *cause* music to happen in the rehearsal room and in performance rather than *make* it happen. Chant truly transforms our musical being *if* we allow it to.

A PEDAGOGICAL JOURNEY

For many, *chant* and *religion* are synonymous words with intersecting meanings. This book details a pedagogy that uses chant to build musical skill and music understanding. For that reason, this text could be considered revolutionary. While chant was used for the expression of belief, it was also a vehicle by which a common musical understanding could be taught and shared. Long before an Edwin Gordon, a

Zoltan Kodaly, or a Lowell Mason, chant crafted a pedagogy for music teaching and learning that was, in essence, devoid of notational restrictions. Notation represented shapes and arcs; chant had not learned to micromanage rhythm. Chant allowed us to experience the bare bones of what is essential to *being* a musician in the truest sense of the word. Chant was our first music method. It provided a clear path to hearing, listening, and experiencing music.

Clarifying the Choral Experience

Some might feel that advocating a return to teaching students chant is a big risk, but I believe it is a risk we must take. I have realized through observing my own students that if we have the courage to learn something new, to learn a notational system that is a bit different from our own, to rely on our ears instead of our eyes, and to allow our listening to guide our musicing with others, then our ensembles will transform themselves. Those who developed chant in the Middle Ages developed a way of making, hearing, and expressing music that, for so many reasons, we should now re-examine for its hidden pedagogical and musical secrets.

Aside from the musical skills that chant teaches (as detailed in this book), it is truly the miracle of a community of musicians bound together through sound and listening that makes the risk worth taking. In an age where communication is instantaneous, to go back several hundred years and revisit a "system" of music making that grew out of a community of people in a common cause assumes new importance. For me, chant merges all that I know about music learning and with all that I believe about the power of what it means for musicians to be together. And above all, chant allows musicians to "take possession"—sole possession of the music in the most organic of ways. And we all know as teachers and conductors that when that truly happens, music speaks in a direct and honest way that is difficult not to hear. When all conditions are right, chant allows us to be alone with sound yet in community with others, which nourishes not only our music making but also our daily lives.

I hope you will take a risk and take the journey we are suggesting here. While I would like to say this is a "new pedagogy," it obviously is not such a "new approach." For some reason—perhaps hundreds of years, perhaps the notation system, or perhaps the fact that chant grew out of liturgical music—chant is thought of as a "dead art." Why we have chosen not to revisit it prior to this has stymied me. At the urging of James Whitbourn, I was pushed over the pedagogical ledge to revisit chant, and it has changed not only me, but all the singers I have had the privilege of working with. Please find the courage to take the risk and teach your students in a way that you were not taught. I can assure you that this risk will reap huge rewards for both you and your students.

Finally, my thanks to my student Isabella Burns, who has led our musical expedition with skill and a pedagogical maturity beyond her years. My thanks to my student Cortlandt Matthews, who painstakingly engraved the chants. And my thanks to Jonathan Palmer Lakeland and John Baker for their work on the chant CD. And finally, my thanks to The Westminster Williamson Voices for trusting this new way of singing together and learning together. For me, the results and our work together speak for themselves. As always, thank you to Linda Vickers, my editor, and to Martha Chlipala, my designer, for the beauty she brings to every book.

—James Jordan
January 2014

WHY IT'S WORTH TAKING THE LEAP TO EMBRACE CHANT

Art allows you to play, express, represent, honor, heal, teach, sanctify, encode and explore ideas. (p. 160)

—Thomas Moore
in *A Religion of One's Own*

These considerations throw new light on the idea that feelings, emotions, moods and the like are cognitive, and that the expression of them must therefore be cognitive too. Drawing on neuroscientific models of brain function, Antonio Damasio hypothesizes that emotions are "somatic markers" of the situations that provoke them. Once moved in a certain way, we see things differently, and in most cases see them better than we could otherwise. There are many situations that cannot be well understood without taking account of the feelings appropriate to them. We reason with such feelings; we interpret with them. But we most often do so in proximity to expressive performatives, the force of which radiates through our language generally and completes the confluence of expression and truth. (p. 69)

—Lawrence Kramer
in *Expression and Truth*

...the cell is an ideal place to learn to know yourself, to search realistically and regularly the process of your own mind and feelings. (p. vii)

…But internal factors may be even more crucial in assessing one's development as a human being. Honesty, sincerity, simplicity, humility, pure generosity, absence of vanity, readiness to serve others— qualities which are within reach of every soul—are the foundation of one's spiritual life. Development in matters of this nature is inconceivable without serious introspection, without knowing yourself, your weaknesses and mistakes…. (pp. 211–212)

—Nelson Mandela
in *Conversations with Myself*

I must admit that I did not initially accept the subject matter of this book. The idea of chant gave me pedagogical "clay feet." For me, chant was something to be admired, but was certainly a bit too complex for even a cursory exploration other than in music history classes. Sound has always been my teacher. Despite the fact that my logic or lack of experience tells me not to pursue something, it is sound that always draws me into a deeper dialogue with myself. Sometimes that dialogue is easy when dealing with simple matters of pedagogy, conducting technique, or rehearsal technique. The more difficult conversations occur when we have to convince ourselves that a drastic turn in how we have done things in the past is warranted. Such dialogues are usually deeply jarring and initially deeply uncomfortable. While I have had these dialogues with myself frequently in my career, I can remember only two other times when I rearranged my "pedagogical DNA" in such a dramatic fashion.

In 1999, I wrote a book entitled *The Musician's Soul*. That book attempted to map out all the "journeys" I was taught by my teachers, which are necessary for an artist to make music in a way that celebrates spirit, caring, and making music together in a deeply meaningful way. That book spoke of the broad brush strokes necessary and the inward landscape that needs to be tilled to serve both the composer and the music. That book not only painted broad themes for personal exploration, but also sought to move artists to be more aware. That book stopped short of practical application, but pointed the way for strong internal self-examination.

To come to the point, chant is the practical application of *all* the major themes in *The Musician's Soul*. While the beginning of anyone's musical journey needs to occur alone in one's silence, at some point as musicians we must bind that experience to the sound we make. The "stuff" for binding spirit into sound must utilize the harnessed power of a community of people who have a desire to deeply listen to each other. The vehicle must have some common dominator of spirit through which all can enter in. While the sound may be the force that moves forward, it is the energy of the spirit that gives a sound its human and communicative power.

Aside from improving listening and ensemble skills with chant, we can gain a new understanding of phrasing and musical line that is natural, that serves the needs of the text and does not take its ideas from a notational system that works against the most beautiful ideas contained in musical line. How to move sound forward is our challenge as musicians. To understand chant is to gain a deep understanding of our choral foundations, our very musical DNA. Through chant, we use our ears to plot our musical trajectories. Chant is not an individual experience but rather the experience of a group of musicians who join together to create an aural architecture of incredible beauty, born out of simplicity.

Standing away as an observer, I watched both James Whitbourn and Isabella Burns teach my singers at the Choral Institute at Oxford to have the courage to chant together using a "new" notation and just simply trust in each other in sound. I witnessed a musical miracle. Through chant, all the things I know we must teach our choirs—pitch, rhythm, expressivity, connection to each other and sound, and empowerment of musical idea through breath—just "happened." Aided and supported by an acoustic that formed a kind of chant "womb," chanting became not only a musical expression for all of us but also a deeply affirming life experience that caused us to find what makes the best music—the most honest human expression.

Nelson Mandela brilliantly distills for us that "honesty, sincerity, simplicity, humility, pure generosity, absence of vanity, readiness to serve others—qualities that are within reach of every soul—are the foundation of one's spiritual life...." Those very qualities need to be at the center of any music pedagogy that hopes to teach not only skill but also artistry. Plainchant does all that and much more.

After many extended conversations with myself, trying to step back and analyze what chanting does for an ensemble, tempered with all the experiences I have mapped out in my pedagogical life in writing and in practice, I have come to the conclusion that there is simply no more direct pedagogical path to understand and sing in this meaningful way than through plainchant. Chant allows us to be alone but with others; chant asks us to make ourselves less so others become more; chant asks us to serve something larger than ourselves; and chant demands us to listen deeply so we always hear what is the best in ourselves. Chant creates a sacred place for communities of singers unlike anything else I know or have ever experienced.

BALANCING ON A FASCINATING PEDAGOGICAL TIGHTROPE

Observance of the soul can be deceptively simple. You take back what has been disowned. You work with what is, rather than what you wish were there. (p. 9)

It is not easy to observe closely, to take the time and to make the subtle moves that allow the soul to reveal itself further. You have to rely on every bit of learning, every scrap of sense, and all kinds of reading, in order to bring intelligence and imagination to the work. (p. 10)

One of the strongest needs of the soul is for community.... (p. 92)

—Thomas Moore
in *Care of the Soul*

I appeal to you therefore, from the outset, not to be discouraged, even though my explanations are somewhat difficult: for without these indispensible first principles we shall never succeed in singing correctly. By the true simplicity of its melodic make-up, both modal and rhythmic, and by the very manner of its composition, Gregorian chant is essentially a delicate construction, which a mere trifle can damage. (p. 7)

—Joseph Gajard
in *The Rhythm of Plainsong*

Soulful expression in music—it can't be recognized by rules. If a theme, a phrase, suddenly says something to you, you don't need to be able to explain. It's suddenly just this gesture that's accessible to you. (p. 6)

—Ludwig Wittgenstein
in Lawrence Kramer,
Expression and Truth

For most of my career, I have had a fascination with music teaching and learning. The rehearsal room presents conductor/teachers with daily challenges to unlock not only the musical elements in a score, but all those things that make music inspirational, uplifting, life affirming and, in some cases, life altering.

Methods and techniques in choral music rightly focus upon the building of music skills. Sight-reading, singing in tune, accurate rhythm, and unified diction and choral ensemble sound are held up as the "sine qui non" of our art. Early in my teaching career, I believed that if one laid all those elements, somehow the "mystery" within the score would be unlocked and revealed.

Many pedagogies that are available for use with choirs of all ages are targeted at literacy and, at times, a type of cultural awareness of the roots of the music. For example, Kodaly not only provided a method with advancing music literacy, but he also exposed students to an incredible world of folk music. Similarly, Carl Orff, through Orff Schulwerk, advanced a similar cultural awareness. Other highly effective methods, such as Music Learning Theory developed and nurtured by Edwin E. Gordon and his many students (this author being one of them), moved students to a deeper appreciation of music through understanding.

Then there are a number of philosophical-based approaches that attempt to grow the inside of the musician. Whether we associate with the ideas of Bennett Reimer and the aesthetic education movement, or the route suggested in *The Musician's Soul* and the series of books that follows culminating in the most recent *The Musician's Trust*, we certainly become aware that part of any conducting/teaching experience must involve the careful construction and building of a musician's interior life. For the most part, the business of music has approached skill and the building of one's interior spiritual space as separate acts to be merged at some point or in some way in performance. And for many of us, that was and is successful.

But what if there was a way to teach musical skill that showed musicians the real connection between spirit and skill—a pedagogy so crafted that skill could not advance without spirit that is built in tandem with musical skill? The excitement I have about this book is that plainchant is, perhaps, the only pedagogy presently available where one aspect of the pedagogy (skill) is deeply dependent and deeply intertwined to the human condition of each singer on a daily basis!

I must also add that I have become deeply troubled of late by persons who believe that the development of "skills" is the be-all and end-all in choral singing. Many years ago, when I studied with Elaine Brown, she would often say that "choirs will sing as they are able to sing." In the early part of my career, I believed that she was referring to their skills. But now I believe that one must develop skill and spirit in tandem and that, perhaps, spirit will *always* trump skill.

My pedagogical excitement surrounding chant and its use, even at a basic level, is that both skill and spirit can and must be developed in tandem. Chant demands us to be aware of our interior selves. Chant demands that we immediately become part of a larger musical community where "less" of the individual becomes "more" for the ensemble. It requires of us at every minute to find our own center, our music-making spacious interior that allows our very being to be human resonators of the sounds we sing and play.

THE TIGHTROPE

That, then, is THE pedagogical tightrope. Skill cannot be developed without a "spiritual" awareness of others, and vice versa. I have long believed that while some repair of intonation and tone can take place on a technical platform in rehearsal, faulty intonation, faulty blend, and other performance issues are as much a problem of spirit, listening, and breathing, even more so than technique. In fact, when such problems are approached technically, the "fixes" usually don't last. Chant requires us to maintain a constant balance between exterior technique and one's interior. It demands that we understand the miracles of people singing with others and the power of listening in *communtatis* with others to be as much a part of our rehearsal procedure as right vowel, count singing, or any other rehearsal procedure we choose to exercise in the moment. Chant requires us always to monitor the balance between applying musical performance "rules" and making sure our being is always right. If accomplished, singers will come to understand quickly how important their "insides" are to the process of being a musician, and artist. It is for that reason that I believe this pedagogy is laden with miracles and human inspiration for all of us.

There are few pedagogies available to choral musicians that can address the skill aspects of our art as well as the deeply important spiritual aspects of that art in the same moment. This book attempts to show you that technique and spirit are the best partners and that we should not develop them separately, assuming one or the other will magically happen. Chant allows us to pedagogically "will" and balance our pedagogical tightrope where skill informs spirit, and vice versa.

PREFACE

James Whitbourn

The practical book which accompanies this volume and is reprinted in full from pages 165 to 230 describes the content on its own cover as 'Essential Chants for all Musicians'. That is not to say that the chants included are the only chants we could have chosen - my collaborator Isabella Burns and I chose from thousands of possible options - but more to say that the knowledge and practice of plainchant itself is an essential tool for musicians in all walks of life - and especially for choral musicians. In my introduction to that collection (pages 171 to 189) I lay out my own journey with chant and my reasons for placing it so high on the list of required tools for all musicians.

The work that James Jordan initiated with his own choir, Westminster Williamson Voices, however, shows that this is not merely a theoretical position but one which bears its fruit in sound and musicianship. After working with chant, phrasing is understood in a quite different way; tuning, sensitivity to rhythmic nuance—all these qualities are naturally embedded into the performance and study of chant. Chant is a ready-made pedagogical tool which already covers most of the disciplines required of choral singers and choral conductors. Just as pianists need to practice scales to reach the top levels of keyboard technique, so singers and choral conductors need to understand how plainchant works. They need also to understand the level of technical and musical skill required to create a well-phrased, shapely, suitably-nuanced choral unison. Our experience shows the study to be transformative and to singers who are open to the subtleties that chant brings, it can be exhilarating.

Appropriate time should be allocated to working with the CD which accompanies this book, for it is only by hearing the manner of phrasing and quality of line which chant offers that you can finally come to its essence. Subtleties that are impossible to notate are inherent in the music itself. While chant sung by a solo voice is telling and informative, it goes without saying that the real work begins when plainchant is brought to choirs, because it is only then that the essence of collaborative music-making within a unison line can be felt. Choral singers are so used to singing in parts and living in their own little world that it is liberating and unifying to make music together outside part writing, in a place where there is equality rather than division between voices.

It is only because all this has been borne out in practice within James Jordan's studio workshops with Williamson Voices that this book exists at all. Were it not the case, we could leave chant as a niche repertoire for liturgical singers. As it is, we have found and proven it to be essential repertoire for every musician.

—James Whitbourn
Oxford, 2014

To the reader: James Whitbourn has also written an important Introduction to the *Laudate* book in Part II of this volume, beginning on page 172. The reader is encouraged to read that Introduction in tandem with the above Introduction.

LIVING THE CHANT

Dominic Gregorio

Renaissance philosophers often said that it is the soul that makes us human. We can turn that idea round and note that it is when we are most human that we have our greatest access to soul. (p. 9)

—Thomas Moore
in *Care of the Soul*

Three years ago while living in India completing my yoga teacher training, I took daily chanting lessons with a teacher named Sangeeta in the ancient holy city of Rishikesh, the birth city of yoga, set upon the banks of the raging legendary Ganges River. As a practitioner of Western chant, I was entranced by the beauty of the melodic modes of the Indian Raga. There are ragas for every season, for calling upon the rain and sun, for sunrise or sunset meditation, for relaxation, or for energy.

I was an impatient student. In my Western conceit, I considered myself an advanced musician. I was, after all, completing a doctoral degree in music. I wanted the information from Sangeeta, and I wanted it all, now. I wanted to write it all down and have it all in front of me. But this is not the way Indian chant is taught or learned; it remains to this day an oral tradition.

It shocked me to be disciplined by my teacher to be patient when I thought I was being a diligent student. She instructed me to stop attempting to notate the chant using the Western musical staff, notes, and bar lines. Most importantly, she admonished me for wanting to learn the next chant when I had not fully embodied the chant we were currently learning. I naively felt that simply knowing the words, notes, and rhythms was enough. It was not. I was missing the essential spiritual character that comes through being with and living the chant. I realized after a few weeks how arrogant and typically Western I was being. I was attempting to learn a foreign spiritual art form by applying my Western set of terminology, expectations, and learning styles.

I came back to Sangeeta and I surrendered myself. I relaxed and I followed her instruction to make my voice one with the harmonium, one with her voice, one with the wisps of fragrant incense. Thinking slowed, sometimes stopped, and the chant penetrated even deeper layers of my being. When I left, I would continue chanting, crossing the walking bridge over the Ganges River, chanting all the way back to the yoga ashram up in the hills, each repetition like the beads of a rosary.

I marveled at how lucky I was to learn in this oral tradition, to learn in the way that chant was originally passed down before notation. Imagine the kind of mind it would take to memorize the catalog of our Western liturgical chants. Imagine the dedication of these specialists living and breathing this life in chant!

Rewind to a decade ago, when I sang for three years in the St. Clement's Church Choir in Philadelphia, Pennsylvania, under Peter Conte. St. Clement's performs the Tridentine Rite, the mass as it was crystallized by the fabled sixteenth-century Council of Trent. A professional choir of sixteen singers performs the Latin mass ordinary and propers and all of the important holy days. At first, I was a nervous wreck, feeling unworthy and still developing the sight-singing skills to be successful in a choir of that caliber.

Nothing lays you bare like plainchant. Eight of us men would sing the Gregorian propers from the *Liber Usualis* each week—each performance a magical act of alignment and concentration. Singing the plainchant each week taught real vulnerability. It was so easy to fail, to be exposed in a moment of broken concentration, to make an error that breaks the concentration of a fellow singer, causing a cascade of errors. When we were all in flow together, in the zone, something was transcended—something rare and beautiful was achieved and experienced.

Entering into the plainchant with a group of singers is like deciding to take an identical journey together, each step identical, each step simultaneous. Is there anything in music, or life, that even closely resembles this?

We live in a world of extreme contrasts, each of us living an experience so different and uniquely ours. In polyphony, even homophony there is harmony, there is difference from part to part. Not so in plainchant. It is a spiritual representation of our inherent oneness. It is the reason why the medieval and renaissance cadence, where two divergent voices become one, is called the *clausula vera*, the "true close." It is a returning back to the One. From Oneness we go, to Oneness we return. To feel together the arsis (the gathering of energy in a phrase) and the thesis (the dissipation of energy) is a feeling like no other. It is an encapsulation of the rollercoaster of our human lives. We are, ultimately, one.

Living the chant each week was spiritually significant for this act of coming together in unison, one voice, amidst the insane modern noisy lives we lead. My choral literature professor at USC, Nick Strimple, would inspire us to imagine what chant or polyphonic music would have sounded like in the sixteenth century, far before electricity, the industrial revolution, cars. Even more so today, it is important to return to chant, the incantation of the stories and spiritual message of our Western heritage. As a new choral music professor, I have yet to program a concert that does not include chant. Having lived chant in various traditions, I feel it necessary for my students to be exposed to its beauty and lessons each semester. We cannot speak to the past, but we can re-experience the flavor of the past in the present moment through singing and living the ancient plainchants.

RICHLY RADIANT:
THE SPIRITUALITY OF CHANT

Steven Pilkington

Renaissance philosophers often said that it is the soul that makes us human. We can turn that idea round and note that it is when we are most human that we have our greatest access to soul. (p. 9)

—Lucian Freud,
one of Britain's greatest modern painters,
in *Lucian Freud: The Studio*

I need to begin with a disclaimer. I am not a musicologist or much of a trained theoretician. I am a college professor and a church musician with more than thirty years' experience in parishes spread across the broad expanse that is America. It has been an exciting if confounding time, as the trajectory of sacred music has changed drastically in the last several decades. Because of my need to train young church musicians and my own desire to grapple with the future of American church music, I have spent many years ruminating on what makes music holy. Admittedly, it has been hard to concentrate, for the roar of rock and the sweetness of pop has drowned out the more solemn tones that traditionally held the worshipper captive in the house of God.

That said, for me, all music is spiritual, as its language seems to reach beyond our physical substance into the emotional sinews where the chemistry of our souls lie. But while music can open our inner selves to a teeming variety of emotional experiences, it is important to note that not all music is holy no matter how deep and far-reaching the resonance may seem. In the words of the great German Romantic poet, Goethe, "The holiness of sacred music, the jocund humor of folk-tunes, are the pivots round which all true music revolves...Worship or dance." (Quoted in S. Langer, *Philosophy in a New Key,* 1942.) In a book concerned with one of the greatest collections of spiritual music ever preserved, I would suggest that understanding what makes music holy is worth exploring for a moment, as it is clear to me that plainchant has little to do with the pulse of dance but is richly radiant with the purest kind of holiness.

In teaching about the holy, I've long employed a definition found in Webster's *Seventh New Collegiate Dictionary.* It seems to me exactly the right language to use when talking about things of a sacred nature, especially as related to music. The entry reads something like this:

1: set apart to the service of God or a god : SACRED
2 a : characterized by perfection and transcendence : commanding absolute
   adoration and reverence b : being spiritually pure : GODLY
3 a : evoking or meriting veneration or awe b : being awesome, frightening, or
   beyond belief

During the early years of the church's formation, its leaders were deeply concerned about the nature of sacred music and the dangers of singing overtly secular music as a part of regular liturgical practice or even after a glass of wine or two. While little has survived regarding the musical customs of the first believers, by the end of the third century one already finds Clement of Alexandria exhorting his readers with significant finger wagging regarding the dangers of pagan songs. Writing in his primer, *The Instructor,* he urged his flock to banish all worldly music:

> Burlesque singing is the close friend of drunkenness.... For if people
> occupy their time with pipes, and psalteries, and choirs, and dances,
> and Egyptian clapping of hands, and such disorderly frivolities,
> they become quite immodest and intractable, beat on cymbals and

drums, and make a noise on instruments of delusion.... And every improper sight and sound...must by all means be excluded; and we must be on guard against whatever pleasure titillates eye and ear, and enervates the soul. For the various spells of the broken strains and plaintive numbers of the Carion muse corrupt men's morals, drawing to perturbation of mind, by the licentious and mischievous art of music.

For denizens of the twenty-first century, his concerns are curiously amusing, for with the mention of clapping of hands, beating on drums and cymbals, the titillation of the eye and ear, and the use of such words as "licentious" and "disorderly frivolities," one is jettisoned into the contentious language of our own time as it relates to recent liturgical discourse.

As ecclesiastical disquietude regarding pagan music is a timeless liturgical theme, it is not surprising then that over the course of centuries, a form of Christian music evolved that, to this day, more than a thousand years since it was codified, seems spiritually pure, holy, otherworldly and, above all, set apart to the service of God. By design and, one assumes, with great intentionality, Gregorian chant became a music that successfully achieved a separation from all that seems profane and worldly. Simone Weil, a French philosopher and political activist widely admired for her Christian mysticism, wrote: "It is quite conceivable that someone who is a passionate music lover might at the same time be evil or corrupt as a person. But I would find it hard to believe that such a thing could be true of anyone who has a thirst for Gregorian chant." It's an interesting idea.

While it was long believed that the origins of Christian liturgical music, especially as related to the singing of the psalms, must have been connected to Jewish ritual practice by a "sacred bridge," today it is thought that the eventual emergence of Gregorian chant came out of the psalmic practices found in early monastic communities. Especially in keeping vigil during the night, the singing of the psalter was a way of managing worldly appetites and focusing the mind on higher spiritual planes. No wonder the entire cycle of 150 psalms became the weekly diet for each week's spiritual sustenance, day and night. The venerable St. Basil (ca. 330–379), Bishop of Caesarea, the Roman capital of Palestine, wrote this regarding the psalter:

> A psalm implies serenity of soul; it is the author of peace, which calms bewildering and seething thoughts. For it softens the wrath of the soul, and what is unbridled it chastens. A psalm forms friendships, unites those separated, conciliates those at enmity. Who, indeed, can still consider him an enemy with whom he has uttered the same prayer to God? So that psalmody, bringing about choral singing, a bond, as it were, toward unity, and joining the people into a harmonious union of one choir, produces also the greatest of blessings, charity. (Taruskin, p. 836, footnote 2)

What better reason for embarking on a musical and spiritual journey with the repertoire of chant than arriving at a place of unity and charity in the choral context?

Dom Jacques Hourlier, a passionate advocate for chant and the author of *Reflections on the Spirituality of Gregorian Chant,* wrote:

> The sacred universe into which Gregorian chant introduces us is the world of prayer—or, if you prefer, of union with God, which is the ultimate goal or aim of prayer. The many reasons for this could be summarized in three characteristics of the chant: spontaneity, depth, and truth.
>
> The chant's spontaneity derives from the almost undefinable aura of purity which it has about it—purity of technique, expression, and intent. Other nuances are simplicity, dignity, and discretion. But these can all be summed up by a single word: humility.
>
> The chant's depth comes from its calm or gravity, which produces serenity and balance. These in turn give rise to an atmosphere filled with gentleness, strength, and peace. It has often been said that Gregorian chant removes us from our ordinary surroundings, makes us lose our bearings, sets us apart. (pp. 46–47)

How remarkable that a modest scale of pitches deployed monophonically achieves the many ends just described. Gregorian phrases do seem to be a kind of true perfection for with a minimum of means, they reach a maximum spiritual effect. Whether propelling one towards interior silence or upwards into joy (as in the "Exsultet," the enduring hymn of praise sung before the paschal candle during the Easter Vigil), one thing remains true: the chant is deeply spiritual because it is profoundly human. A simple story follows:

On a recent Sunday afternoon I was headed to meet a friend for coffee. While one might think Manhattan is a narrow island, moving across town in a cab can often be one of New York's most frustrating experiences. Ten blocks or less can seem like driving across a small state—especially if you're late and in a hurry. If there's a lot of traffic, it can take several lights just to go half a block. Unfortunately, it's not unusual to get in a cab thinking the traffic looks light and two blocks later you're slammed by a snarl of traffic. Too far to get out and quickly walk to one's destination but slow enough to make the blood rise towards the boiling point inside the cab. Hope springs eternal that the traffic will clear in another block. I was having one of these experiences when out of my fog of New York resentment I noticed some incredibly beautiful music wafting into the back seat. It was the singing of a solo male voice, rich, resonant, hypnotic, unaccompanied by instruments or choir, and with the rise, fall, and cadence of Gregorian chant. Rather than sleep-inducing (as I often find chant CDs to be), the music was actually compelling, even gripping, not only because of the fervid singing, but because of the lavish deployment of melodic ornamentation around the play of pitches. The more carefully I listened, the more engrossed I became in what I determined to be a highly spiritualized sound.

I was actually shocked when the cab driver looked over the partition and asked if I was going to get out. I'd been lost in my taxi's soundscape (only in New York) and, unnoticed, had arrived at my destination. A brief conversation ensued with the driver. It was indeed holy music I had been listening to but not from the Christian tradition. What I had been immersed in was the cantillation of a chapter from the

Qu'ran (Koran). I was surprised: surprised to be hearing sacred text while dashing to a date, surprised by a shared Islamic experience in a cab, and astonished at the simple but mesmerizing beauty of a sound that I knew instinctively to be sacred. I was also excited to learn that the cabdriver was not playing the radio but an app called Muslim Pro. By the end of my first cup of coffee, it was installed on my iPhone and I was eager to get back on the street so I could pop in my ear buds and explore this captivating sound further.

Like most of the hundreds of Latin-texted Gregorian chants, I could not understand the meaning of the Qu'ran recitation without a printed translation, yet I had a powerful sense of its sacred content. What is in the sound of chanted music when wed to sacred text that seems so holy? Why does unmetered, modal monophony, unmediated by instruments and attached to Holy Writ come out sounding sacred even when the language itself is incomprehensible?

Nearly every religious tradition makes use of some kind of chant as sung prayer. One of my favorite CD collections is *Chant: Spirit in Sound, The Best of World Chant.* Therein is recorded, among many offerings, Sufi devotional music; a Sanskrit chant from the Hindu tradition; a Zuni sunrise song; haunting Armenian monophony wed to music played by the duduk, one of the world's oldest wind instruments made from apricot wood and dating to 1200 BC; medieval pilgrim songs from the monastery of Montserrat in Spain; and Tibetan-style overtone singing accompanied by indigenous bells of surpassing beauty. The array of sounds from many cultures with their varied understandings of pitch and what comprises a scale is inspirational, although I would add, in support of the idea that unaccompanied, unmetered monophony is one of the purest expressions of the sacred, that whenever a percussive or melodic instrument is added into the mix, no matter how beguiling the color or effect, the music does seem to become more earthbound and less ethereal. The same holds true when the pulse becomes regularized, the measured pace more reflective of the human impulse to move to a beat and organize time rather than disappear into the timelessness of eternity.

One answer to these questions concerning the sacredness of chant lies in the purity and beauty of expression that surfaces when people sing, especially in a corporate manner. I believe the human voice is the best, most refined of all musical instruments and, as expressed by Henry Wadsworth Longfellow, "The human voice is the organ of the soul." "Of all the sounds which music utters," writes another nineteenth-century author in *The New York Review* (1838), "none are so pleasing, so varied, so capable of affecting the feelings, so refined and delicate and at the same time overpowering, as the human voice." He continues:

> A single voice with the compass of only two octaves can express
> more than any instrument or any combination of instruments.
> Compared indeed with the tones of an instrument, the human voice
> seems like life contrasted with inanimate nature. In singing, a soul
> seems to enter into sound and to give it life. This effect indeed,
> is partially produced by an instrument in the hands of a skillful
> performer, though never in a degree equal to the power of voice.
> (Lambert Lilly, *The New York Review*, 1838, p. 46, Google Books)

As for what happens when personal religious experience is screwed to the emotional core from whence deeply felt singing emanates, I recently had an epiphany. It involves the telling of a tale related to my teaching life. Part of my responsibilities at the college involves supervising some of the Westminster undergraduates in their church positions. Typically each student makes a video recording of his or her midweek rehearsal, which we then review together back on campus. It's a great way to teach: survey the action, stop the clock; discuss what happened; review again; set goals for future observations.

One of my students comes out of the Pentecostal tradition. A gifted musician with a winsome passion for all choral music, he's been shy about bringing in recordings of his rehearsals with his church choir, unlike in previous semesters when he always had ready footage of his other choir, the campus group he founded as a freshman. After one viewing of his church rehearsal, I understood his hesitation. This group was a slice of real life: made up of untrained volunteers, mostly the age of his parents, his work with them was mainly accomplished by rote. On view was a painstakingly slow process, literally note by note, a kind of call and response, a back and forth between the director and each section of the choir. No piano to drill the parts, just voice to voice communication. But, oh, the sound! Here was a vocal furnace of impassioned singing—not loud or crude, just resonant with the deep conviction of faith and the untutored power of the natural voice. I suspect my student felt the rest of the class would be somewhat appalled at both the penetrating sound and the process. But the response from his fellow students was enthusiastic and clamorous. What was striking to all of us was this opportunity to observe the ancient practice of oral transmission being accomplished in an ordinary, everyday environment. It felt holy and wholesome.

How is this story related to the spirituality of chant? The singing of chant throughout the medieval period (the fifth through the fifteenth centuries) was the occupation of thousands and thousands of men and women living in close community. For at least half a millennium, it was a tradition created and passed down by oral transmission, a process that surely included some improvisation and experimentation as any oral tradition does until it is codified and published (and rigor mortis threatens to set in). It was also a musical miracle, for its creativity and beauty formed a daily soundtrack of astounding variety and durability for the extensive liturgical life of the church. With the eight daily offices and daily Mass (sometimes several masses on special days), and the many festal days that marked moments from the life of Christ and the numerous saints of the Church, the singing of Latin chant became nearly a full day's work that also spilled into part of the night. (Matins or Vigils was sung during the night and Lauds before dawn, both offices being substantial liturgical units filled with great responsories, long canticles, hymns, and many psalms with antiphons.) As St. Benedict ordered his monastic brothers' life, he reminded them that all this activity was the opus dei, "the work of God." By the end of the medieval period, the entire chant corpus consisted of thousands of monophonic pieces that supported the cycle of daily prayer, the weekly circuit of the full psalter with antiphons, and the larger cycles marking Christ's birth and resurrection—wheels within wheels within wheels to use a favored medieval and quite cosmic metaphor.

Here was a music for believers, a ritual music of faith, a daily response to the stories and events found in the Bible, the Christian family album as it were. The spirituality of chant cannot be disconnected from this power source. As I observed my student's work with his church choir and listened to their sound as he labored to teach the music of black gospel, this was the lesson of which I was reminded. While theological assent is obviously not necessary for the art of singing or performing chant, it is essential, I believe, to have an understanding of the theological wellspring out of which this wondrous repertoire flowed to more fully enter into its spiritual beauties. I have two points to make in this regard, one concerning a theology of "otherness" and one concerning sound:

First, chant functions principally as a vehicle for the ceremonial declamation of sacred Latin texts, whether sung by a single soloist, a small group, a trained choir or, perhaps in the earliest centuries, the entire congregation. These texts, mostly made of psalmic fragments pieced together to form a highly sophisticated commentary, address God, the object of worship. This is in contrast to much of today's worship (outside of the Catholic context), which is generally a people-centered affair surrounded by a music that is highly personal, devotional, and emotive. In classic medieval theology, humankind gives praise and thanksgiving to God alone through the liturgy. Worship is about God's "worth"-ship. It is understood that God is present and that he bestows his grace on those who have gathered to worship him. God is hymned through songs of adoration because he is above all things, a transcendent, cosmic creator distinct from the universe itself. God is thanked and glorified for his mighty, unimaginable acts, and most especially for the gift of his Son who redeemed all of creation through self-sacrifice. Praising, thanking, and beseeching God are all accomplished through prayers, sacred readings, and ritual acts. Through chants that have been carefully honed and polished over time, selected sentences are enhanced by a music that exudes a purified, unearthly air. Such otherworldly music is deemed appropriate, as God is spirit, immaterial. In this sense, the music becomes like an icon, a window or passageway into another unseen, supernatural world.

I love that the word *neume*—the term for the primary strokes used in chant notation—actually derives from the Greek word *pneuma,* which means "air in motion, breath, wind," a perfect nomenclature for spirit-driven music. How lovely that the *porrectus*—a three-note neume that uses a swooping curve to connect two of its pitches—looks like a small gust of wind. The word also means "gesture," as in a melodic movement of the voice that might cover a note, a short phrase, or even an extended melisma, all through coursing air. Additionally, *inspire* is also the root of the word *inspiration,* meaning both drawing in air—the breath of life itself—as well as being filled with a positive, uplifting feeling. The use of a dictionary definition charts the word *inspire* in this clarifying manner:

> ORIGIN Middle English enspire, from Old French inspirer, from
> Latin inspirare "breathe or blow into," from in- "into" + spirare
> "breathe." The word was originally used of a divine or supernatural
> being, in the sense "impart a truth or idea to someone."

In this profound way, when we speak of the spirituality of chant, we actually mean "breathing in the spirit," as well as "inspiration" through the combined use of scripture and monody to "impart a truth or idea to someone."

Integral to the medieval liturgy as breath itself, the glory of chant lies in its sonic beauty, which, when combined with other non-verbal components (such as stained glass, soaring architecture, incense, bells, richly adorned vestments and ritual vessels, gold, silver, and precious jewels), finds God immanent even as transcendence occurs. In this sense, the singing of chant almost becomes sacramental, the musical experience being a way of reaching out to the Divinity who is no more to be comprehended in words than in music but is nonetheless mystically present in the beauty of holiness.

As Elias Amidon, a spiritual leader speaking from the Sufi tradition, once observed, "What's great about chanting is that it cuts free from the volumes and libraries full of mysticism and words trying to say the ineffable. It's the real thing." (Robert Gass on "Chanting")

This brings me back to my student's choir and my second point. While most gospel singing is not chanting—although I would draw many parallels between the originally monophonic, unaccompanied, orally transmitted Negro spiritual and the development of medieval plainsong—the sound his women produced was "the real thing."

My point is simple: When singing the Gregorian repertoire, it is worth considering its long development as an orally transmitted music sung from the heart, by heart. Wherever the sound of chant is heard, whether in Sioux City, Iowa, or Varanasi, India, or Ho Chi Minh City, Vietnam, the singers are not likely to be holding a book or a piece of paper or a service leaflet. The chant will be sung from memory as most sacred music is performed in the many religious cultures found around the globe. The value of internalizing any sacred repertoire cannot be overestimated, in my opinion, and possibly speaks to the reason why chant notation, even of the simplest form, was so long in appearing. It may have been deemed a superfluous need and even deleterious to the spiritual process of learning to chant of divine things. A story from Charles Ives, one of America's greatest composers, regarding his father's way of making music makes the point in a poignant way:

> [There was] something about the way Father played hymns. Even
> if some of the choir could read music readily at the rehearsals,
> he always liked to play each part over with his horn, and have
> them get it entirely through listening, through the ear, through
> his phrasing, tone, and general style of playing. He had the gift of
> putting something in the music which meant more sometimes than
> when some people sang the words. (Memos, p. 46)

As regards literacy, one can only guess as to how many monks and nuns actually read the texts they were learning since such a skill was not yet a birthright. Even as early as the latter half of the fourth century, one finds St. John Chrysostom, the Archbishop of Constantinople and an important Early Church Father, exulting in the triumph of chanting psalmody in the liturgical context as an invaluable tool for implanting scripture inside human souls:

> In church when vigils are observed David [meaning the psalms] is
> first, middle, and last. At the singing of the morning canticles David
> is first, middle, and last. At funerals and burials of the dead again
> David is first, middle, and last. O wondrous thing! Many who have
> no knowledge of letters at all nonetheless know all of David and
> can recite him from beginning to end. (Taruskin, p. 10)

Of various other factors, I want to remind those leading performances of chant that long before this music was codified and fixed with notation, it was sung by local men and women who had not undergone years of vocal training (as far as we know). Especially away from great urban centers, I'm guessing the sound was often full, faith-filled, perhaps ragged and rugged, and most likely ablaze with color. And, like any oral tradition, when a singer is either bored or inspired, improvisation is only a breath away.

I've recently had my ears roused to the exceptional power of chant when sung fully on the breath and with the natural color of the voice blended into a fully resonating body of choral sound through the work of Marcel Pérès. This French conductor and scholar along with his Ensemble Organum have been investigating the potential connections between various kinds of chant and folk music. His recording from 1985 of Old Roman chant is a revelation (Old-Roman Chant, 7th–8th Centuries, Byzantine Period. Ensemble Organum, directed by Marcel Pérès, Harmonia Mundi HMC 1218). Typically, Old Roman is an ornate style of plainchant that survives in manuscripts from Rome of the late eleventh century. While the earliest surviving Gregorian manuscripts date to two centuries earlier, none of them come from Rome.

Some scholars believe the ornateness of the chant is evidence of a long development connected to the more grand and sophisticated ritual of the Byzantine church and the Greek roots out of which it was formed. Playing with these ideas, Pérès brings to his performances elements that, in advance of hearing them, I can relate as thrilling. Working with renowned Greek cantor Lycourgos Angelopoulos, the Latin chant is wed to a Greek technique of vocal production and to the use of *ison*—a drone employed below the chant line—and the extensive use of microtonal ornamentation. As scholar David Hiley writes, "There is every reason for experimenting with these techniques, for engaging a Greek psaltis [cantor] to sing sections of the chant, for using a flexible rhythm with many 'ornamental' cells flung off rapidly, for cultivating an imperiously open-throated style of vocal delivery with a dynamic level from *mezzo-forte* to *fortissimo* (sample the overwhelming crescendo through the verses and repeats of Alleluia Pascha nostrum, leaving one with feelings of worm-like unworthiness before the splendor and majesty of the divine mystery)." (*Early Music*, February 1987, p. 119) His other recordings of various chant traditions and the earliest polyphony of the church are all radical, ear grabbing, and heart stopping. His creativity will stimulate yours.

For me, it is enough that the limited evidence as to performance practice is far from conclusive regarding any kind of uniformity in style. Even the earliest notational markings (beginning in the ninth century) above or below the text are not always clear as to what the intentions of the scribe were as related to pitch, let alone rhythm. Hiley cites this medieval definition of the *porrectus* (named above): "This sign signifies that the voice first descends and then re-ascends. The second note may be lower than the first by any interval sanctioned by St. Gregory, as also the third note may be higher than the second by the same intervals." (p. 184) It sounds like my grandmother describing her recipe for a heavenly risotto, which may or may not have included turkey stock instead of chicken, perhaps unsalted butter, but regularly with the addition of a thyme sprig unless it was in the winter.... Certainly the rhythmic interpretation of chant is an area of great ambiguity. Only rarely does one find hints that chant may have been rhythmically differentiated. Yet in the St. Gall manuscript (one of three completely notated books with the chants for the Mass from the end of the ninth century), one finds such notes as these: c = celeriter, quickly; p = pressio, driving forward; t = trahere, drag; f = cum fragore, with hard attack; and k = klange, with ringing tone.

Ultimately, what is crucial, I believe, is that the chant is sung from the heart, with the freedom and confidence that comes from performing music from memory, and with an openness and honesty that sounds of humility and vulnerability. After all, one is resurrecting, giving breath and life, to one of the most extraordinary bodies of spiritual music ever wrought for a Divinity.

I end this essay with another observation from Charles Ives. In reflecting on his spiritual experiences, he said, "I remember, when I was a boy—at the outdoor Camp Meeting services in Redding—all the farmers, their families and field hands, for miles around, would come afoot or in their farm wagons. I remember how the great waves of sound used to come through the trees."

Of the singers, he observed:

> It was the way this music was sung that made them big or little—and I had the chance of hearing them big. And it wasn't the music that did it, and it wasn't the words that did it, and it wasn't the sounds (whatever they were—transcendent, peculiar, bad, some beautifully unmusical)—but they were sung "like the rocks were grown." The singers weren't singers, but they knew what they were doing—it all came from something felt, way down and way up....

When I am listening to chant or teaching it to my choir, it is this quality of sound, a purity and naturalness of expression anchored to an inner core of conviction, that I am searching for. As a group, we are always trying to reach down and rise up.

I conclude with these beautiful words from Robert Gass, a great lover of chant:

> At this very moment, the deep and ancient sounds of sacred chant fill churches, temples, mosques, ashrams, and kivas as people join their voices in communal worship. In forests and fields, by the sea and on mountaintops, as the sun rises and falls into dusk, women and men add their chanting voices to the symphony of natural sounds. In the grace before meals and the quiet moments before bed, at marriages and the great transitions of births and deaths, people join together to chant their prayers. At workshops and wellness centers, in hotel ballrooms and the privacy of living rooms, people in cultures where traditional forms have lost their meaning are rediscovering the power of chant.

To this I simply add, thank God.

PART I

We are not human beings having a spiritual experience.
We are spiritual beings having a human experience. (p. 13)

—Pierre Teilhard de Chardin
in Thomas Moore,
A Religion of One's Own

PHOTO: JAMES JORDAN.

EAST ALTER WINDOW BY MARC CHAGALL IN ALL SAINTS', TUDELEY, TONBRIDGE, UK.

CHAPTER 1
INTRODUCTION:
COMMUNITAS

It is strange that truth has to be felt as well as thought. (p. 81)

> —Elaine Brown
> in *Lighting a Candle*

He who has realized that sun and stars and souls do not ramble in a vacuum will keep his heart in readiness for the hour when the world is entranced.

For things are not mute: the stillness is full of demands, awaiting a soul to breathe in the mystery that all things exhale in their craving for communion. (p. xi)

> —Abraham Joshua Heschel
> in David Steindl-Rast
> *Music of Silence*

It means not only *how* and *what* we sing but for whom and *with* whom. (p. 73)

Communication is a thing of spirit, not just voices. A real sharing is not role playing. (p. 74)

The action and the heart go together. (p. 75)

When music becomes the yeasting force for creative teaching and learning, for life itself, it will never be replaced. (p. 80)

> —Elaine Brown
> in *Lighting a Candle*

He may begin by reacting only to outward impressions, and probably refer to these as theater or folklore. But then, little by little, the neums transform him—the music passes from the outside to the inside. Without his being aware of it, or maybe in spite of himself, the chant casts its wonderful spell on him. You called this stage "interiorization,".... (p. 8)

Many of the above thoughts suggest that Gregorian chant is a way of life, as some of you aptly put it. To begin with, the chant helps you to become a more authentic person. It is deeply spiritual because it is profoundly human. (p. 11)

Gregorian chant helps us to understand that listening is a fundamental aspect of spiritual life... A triple role is assigned to the chant: listening, experiencing, edifying. (p. 13)

Listening obliges us to direct our attention outward, to things other than the self, while our voice becomes the instrument of conscience. (p. 17)

The chant's depth comes from its calm or gravity, which produces serenity and balance. These in turn give rise to an atmosphere filled with gentleness, strength, and peace. It has often been said that Gregorian chant removes us from our ordinary surroundings, makes us lose our bearings, sets us apart. Dom Gajard described it as an "interiorizing" effect: we enter into ourselves, not for any introspective self-analysis, but in order to rediscover the One who dwells within us. (p. 47)

—Dom Jacques Hourlier
in *Reflections on the Spirituality of Gregorian Chant*

Notation, far from being the final goal of musical science, is not even a part of it. (p. 117)

—Aristoxnes
from Dom Daniel Saulnier,
Gregorian Chant

Sometimes the most obvious things are the most difficult to see either because they are so simple that they defy discovery or because they have moved beyond our pedagogical sight for many reasons. This is a book I would have never envisioned writing. For me, chant was a part of my music history studies, and as a choral conductor, I knew it was somewhat important to what we do as choral conductors. That is what I was always told, and I accepted the historical role chant played in my studies of music history. Like so many of us, I also studied, taught, and performed the great choral works that are a central part of our repertoire: Durufle, Lauridsen, Martin, Stravinsky, Poulenc, among others. I thought I "understood" chant.

In the summer of 2013, Westminster Choir College inaugurated the *Choral Institute at Oxford*, housing itself within St. Stephen's House, one of the halls of Oxford University. My friend and colleague, James Whitbourn, who helped plan and implement this program, built into the pedagogical fiber of that program a rather considerable plainchant component in addition to the daily singing of evening Compline. When I questioned him about what I considered to be an unusually heavy dose of chant, he told me to trust him on the matter—which I did, but somewhat reluctantly. In a later e-mail correspondence, James explained that from his perspective not only was chant a necessary understanding for conductors and all those involved with choral music, but as he told me, "It is our DNA."

To come to the point, my experience at Oxford was life changing and deeply transformative for not only myself, but for all who attended. In the months since, I have tried to analyze from a pedagogical perspective those experiences. We wrote this book not only to analyze and identify what we learned together, but also to advocate for choral musicians to return to the wisdom of those who developed chant not only as a communal/spiritual act, but also as a means for developing musical skill to express what is at the core of human expression.

Revisiting the Pedagogical Wisdom of Chant

As many of you know, I base most of what I do in rehearsal on the things I learned from Edwin Gordon and the foundational principles that Music Learning Theory teaches us. My first realization is that chant was truly our first music learning theory—an aural art first and foremost that developed not only ear, but also deeply honest music sensibilities. Allow me to briefly describe all of the objectives in music teaching and learning that chant accomplishes:

- Listening to others
- Experiencing musical line in its most exposed and honest context
- Bringing singers to understand simplicity and honesty in a musically and socially complex world
- Awareness of resting tone and modality
- Understanding the DNA of phrasing as carried by text
- Establishment of consistant tempo

> To state the obvious, the essential, fundamental characteristic of Gregorian chant is its pure monophony. Whether the melody is syllabic, ornate, or melismatic, the style always remains linear. Gregorian Chant is totally melodic because it excludes any and all concomitant sounds. The relationship between notes is strictly successive. More than any other type of music—and better, perhaps than any other monophonic musical form—it seems to be aiming at something, or driving at something. In its progression, it never pauses to savor the "present moment" (in contrast to vertical types of music). (p. 39)
>
> —Dom Jacques Hourlier
> in *Reflections on the Spirituality of Gregorian Chant*

- Understanding the need for breathing together
- Singing chant and plainsong teaches musicianship from a harmonic rather than a melodic perspective
- Developing ensemble skills
- Chant creates a sacred place for rehearsing and musicing

Sensitivity overrides sentimentality, and sensitivity leads to contemplation. Note as well that freedom is not license: preexisting conventional forms impose a pattern which is automatically conducive to the elevation of souls. (p. 46)

—Dom Jacques Hourlier
in *Reflections on the Spirituality of Gregorian Chant*

- Gaining an aesthetic for melodic shaping and melodic beauty that is honest and unencumbered.
- Building aural skills by singing within tonic, subdominant, and dominant harmonic structures
- Trust of others

To be sure, there are many excellent volumes on the history and the performance of chant. Their perspective taken from a liturgical point of reference is both valuable and necessary for our consideration. But this book attempts to rotate the perspective of our thinking about chant from a liturgical point of view toward a vision of using chant to build human and musical skills within a choral ensemble. This book is proposing that *plainchant is the foundation upon which musicianship and musical skill is built.* This book is proposing that *chant is the fundamental pedagogy to be employed to teach audiation.* In many ways, while what we are proposing is somewhat a given if you have experienced and performed chant, I have found that shedding new light with a bit of analytical dissection provides not only a new pedagogical path, but clarified insights.

I am convinced because of my work with Edwin Gordon that any worthwhile pedagogy builds on the past. But the problem in music education now is that our pedagogical memories are very short. In fact, many of our best pedagogies revisit concepts that have been in place for hundreds of years. What is fascinating about chant is that it has always been there for us to pedagogically harvest. Its miracles are just beyond our pedagogical sight lines. Music education and theory pedagogy have crafted "new" approaches to teaching this or that. But what is so shocking is that chant contains all we really need to teach and know. Buried within its monophony are all the skills we strive to teach to our choral ensembles—all there for harvesting.

James Whitbourn commented that it is important to "get this right"—that is, to detail as many steps in a pedagogy for teaching chant without causing the experience of chant to lose its effectiveness. I want to get as much "right" as I can, but I am equally passionate about setting out the important ideas contained within singing chant so those ideas become a way of doing things and teaching things in all our choral rehearsals.

Earlier we stated that chant is the "DNA" of everything we do as choral musicians. But just like DNA, there is a difference between acknowledgment that it exists and analysis of its genetic make-up. This book ventures into, or rather re-visits, what exactly lies beneath the surface of chant. As you will see, the principles that modern music learning espouses is embedded in the DNA of chant. All we must do as conductors is to acknowledge what is buried within and use the original source to not only improve the musicianship of our singers, but to create a heightened sense of community and what it means to truly sing together through chant. A sense of deepened personal "being" and perhaps the accessing of a calm and centered spiritual presence will be a natural outgrowth of this suggested pedagogical process.

This will take courage on your part. Chant, because of its sonic "bare bones," leaves one a bit vulnerable to elements of pitch, rhythm, and intonation, and forces one to breathe with others, to enter into musical community, and to be carried by one's ears as one sings. For those who are courageous, the singing of their ensembles will go beyond what they ever could have imagined. And because of that, it is worth the risk.

> What indeed is this communitas? It keeps appearing as a togetherness that seeks the whole universe as its boundary. (p. 31)
>
> —Edith Turner
> in *Communitas*

CHAPTER 2
INDWELLING:
TEACHING THE BEAUTY
OF SIMPLICITY AND CALM

First, silence makes us pilgrims. Secondly, silence guards the fire within. Thirdly, silence teaches us to speak. (p. 1)

—Henri J. M. Nouwen
in *The Way of the Heart*

Unison singing also has a symbolic significance. The singing of only one melodic line signifies the unanimity of spirit and is the symbol of intimate fellowship. (p. 152)

—Wilhelm Ehmann
in *Choral Directing*

You may not be aware that your heart isn't open. You may imagine that you are loving and available when you are not. In this matter, your self-image as an open person may be a cover for your failure to truly open your heart to be influenced and connected. (p. 109)

—Thomas Moore
in *A Religion of One's Own*

The responsive singing of chant in each hour helps monks to find the elusive now dimension of our lives. Chant primes us to respond to the call of each hour; for real living happens not in clock time, not in chronological time (from the Greek chronos), but in what the Greeks called the kairos, time as opportunity or encounter. We live in the now by attuning ourselves to the calls of each moment, listening and responding to what each hour, each situation, brings. (p. 5)

—David Steindl-Rast
in *Music of Silence*

All human language about the spiritual, yes, even the divine language of Holy Scriptures, is essentially transferred from metaphorical language. This is quite in order and corresponds to the order of things and of existence, even though man is spirit from the moment of birth…. (p. 199)

—Soren Kierkegaard
in *Works of Love*

The head and heart cannot function without a unifying principle. That principle is to be found at the crossroads through which each element must pass. That crossroad stands at—and is—the center.

—James Conlon
from the Foreword of *Toward Center*

Centering, which I discuss in this book, is a severe and thrilling discipline, often acutely unpleasant. In my own efforts, I become weak, discouraged, exhausted, angry, frustrated, unhappy, and confused. But someone within me is resolute, and I try again. Within us lives a merciful being who helps us to our feet however many times we fall. (p. 8)

—M. C. Richards
in *Centering*

In order to become attentive to beauty, we need to rediscover the art of reverence. Our world seems to have lost all sense of reverence. We seldom even use the word any more. The notion of reverence is full of riches that we now need desperately. Put simply, it is appropriate that a human being should dwell on this earth with reverence. (p. 31)

—John O'Donohue
in *Beauty: The Invisible Embrace*

One of the stunning revelations that has come from realizing the value of "ensemble chant" (for lack of a better term) is that singing chant is simply not possible without a centered, calm presence. Chant simply will not sing, and chant will not sing in tune without a certain calmness and centeredness of spirit. In the initial stages of using chant to begin each rehearsal, it became clear that unless we did something as a group on some days to "center" and calm ourselves, the result was that the chant did not sing in any dimension. Sound was agitated, even edgy; ensemble members had difficulty singing in tune in a true unison, and the energy in the breath was dispersed and scattered. Certain rehearsal required more "preparation" prior to chanting.

Richard Rohr, in *Immortal Diamond*, used the word "indwelling"[1] to describe that inner landscape that needs to be created and prepared when singing and experiencing chant. Gerard Manley Hopkins called it "inscape," that deeply personal inner landscape that one needs to know about oneself. One of the remarkable lessons my singers learned in experiencing chant is that they acquired an acute awareness about everyone around them while at the same time being acutely aware of themselves. This inner and outer awareness is a necessary skill for musical artistry, yet few if any pedagogies address it, let alone prescribe a way for getting there.

---

1   Richard Rohr, *Immortal Diamond*, p. 121.

To recognize one's indwelling, one must be in a heighted state of awareness of *both* sound and the community of others within which one is singing. When singing chant, singers become acutely aware of others. They become acutely aware of when they themselves are "more" than others either in sound or energy. They become acutely aware of how sound is moving forward and how they fit into the communal sound. We also learned that without the "indwelling" being set, the singing of chant proved more challenging to find each day. In essence, it is a place identified by a sense of calm simplicity.

> Not known, because not looked for
> But heard, half heard in the stillness
> Between two waves of the sea.
> Quick now, here, now, always---
> A condition of complete simplicity
> (Costing not less than everything)
>
> —T. S. Eliot
> in *Four Quartets* from *"Little Gidding"*

In *Toward Center,* my co-author Nova Thomas and I tried to describe, based upon the centering concepts of M. C. Richards, what centering is for artists and how to obtain it. In attempting to describe Center, I summarized the characteristics of "being centered" in the following way:

- Center provides a physical grounding of one's energies, making them strong, undiluted, and immediately transferable to others.
- Center provides a focal point of one's energies; with such focus, those energies can be channeled at will to the musical task at hand.
- Having a strong center minimizes or eliminates tension that causes multiple problems for artists.
- Center provides THE most direct line of communication from the artist outward.
- Honest and sincere artistry cannot occur without Center.
- Center allows for the correct use of the body. Center places one at an anatomical advantage.

- A constant awareness of one's Center becomes an enabler for all things artistic.
- Center has limited effect upon art until it is revealed to others. A person may have a centeredness to oneself, but one must want to connect and share that Center with others.
- Center must be projected or propelled. When a person is centered, it takes channeled energy to transmit the power of that Center to others.
- When a person is truly centered, and that Center is grounded, one usually feels as if one has "lost control." This feeling of losing control to Center should be the goal for all artists.

Toward Center attempted to describe ways of accessing Center, as described above. The hope of that book was that if artists understood what Center was, that awareness would, in some way, guide them to its access, with no specific pedagogy other than the centering practice of Qigong, detailed later in this chapter, which is used as a "preparation" for chant practice.

BEING IN A SACRED SPACE AND PLACE

One of the by-products of using chant as a daily musical "ritual" is that it prepares the rehearsal space in both a personal and somewhat sacred way. I don't believe that conductors always do enough to bring their ensembles to the realization that their rehearsal room must be a sacred place. A place where chances can be taken. A place that both acknowledges and rejoices in the community of being together in sound. For me and my ensemble, the elements that any of us ascribed previously to in "being a musician" are all deeply cultivated and nourished by a daily practice of chant. It perhaps is no secret that monastic communities were bound together by this want to access and achieve a communal spirituality. The desire of community and its inherent wisdom sought in monastic communities is not unlike what we strive for in our ensembles. We cannot achieve such community by talking about its importance. We can only achieve this by daily practice of singing together. The power of many singing in unison together is the representation in sound of a group that is truly "in ensemble." The sacred in each one of us is revealed when we chant. And more importantly, as Frank Battisti tells us in the quote below, we begin to make music in an intimate emotional capacity...we must do it in the same way as "God makes trees."

> A musician is musical when their music making elicits an emotional response from players and listeners. To be musical is to "make music like God makes trees"—that is, in a manner and style that is natural and consistent with the performer's personality, intellect and intimate emotional capacity. Being musical is more than juggling notes; it's liberating what's *inside* the notes. One's music making should awaken the soul.
>
> —Frank Battisti from Eugene Migliaro Corporon, "Principles for Achievement, Enhancing Musicianship and Valued Colleagues," in *Teaching Music through Performance in Band, Vol. 8*

> When imagination is allowed to move to deep places, the sacred is revealed. The more different kinds of thoughts we experience around a thing and the deeper our reflections go as we are arrested by its artfulness, the more fully its sacredness can emerge. (p. 289)
>
> —Thomas Moore
> in *Care of the Soul*

ABANDONMENT OF SELF AND TRUSTING OTHERS

> The art of non-resistance. One gives up the persona, as Yeats would say, and takes up the mask. That is to say, one becomes that which one is not. Free where one is bound. The physics is clear. The way to center is abandonment. (p. 141)
>
> —M. C. Richards
> in *Centering*

One of the lessons learned from our chanting experience in both Oxford and back on campus with the Williamson Voices is that singers had to give up varying amounts of "control" in order to chant together. We quickly discovered that if one person energized the breath, then all one we had to do was "let go" and allow the shape of the line and the melismas to determine the trajectory of the phrase. This is easier stated than taught. I mention once again that through chant, we begin to trust others. My students learned somewhat quickly that once they gave of themselves to something larger than themselves, the music spoke in a stunning, even captivating way. For us, this was the hardest lesson. Many ensembles sing and play well through the gauze of control: control by conductor, control by stronger singers. But we must remember that if we are to elevate our musicians to the miracles of ensemble musicing, then we must find a way to teach them through sounds what it means to truly sing in ensemble. Because of the unison nature of chant, there is no hiding in complex harmonic events. Intonation snares back at our ears when someone is not "in sync" with the energy, sound, or breath in the room. What I witnessed firsthand with my ensemble is that they learned more about musical line and singing together through chant than I could have ever taught them.

CHANT AND THE DEEP CULTIVATION OF IMAGINATION

Imagination is spiritual perception. Authenticity is spiritual presence. We can think of authenticity as the quality of expression, and imagination appears as the realm of the Source, what authenticity draws upon. Or the other way around: authenticity gives impulse, imagination gives us the image. We need the courage of authenticity to carry the originality of imagination into expression. Whichever way you want to figure it, imagination and authenticity are double doors to creation.

—M. C. Richards

QIGONG PRACTICE:
BALANCING ENERGY AND GAINING AWARENESS OF BREATH

> The three intentful corrections, [1. Align the body, 2. Engage the breath, 3. Focus the mind], also known as the three regulations, the three adjustments, or three focal points, are the bedrock of every form of Qigong and Tai Chi. You will notice that to take a deep breath, you must adjust your posture. You will notice that to adjust your posture, it helps to take a deep breath. Once you adjust the posture and the breath, it becomes natural to relax and clear the mind/consciousness. (p. 32)

—Roger Jahnke
in *The Healing Promise of Qi*

> This is the first, wildest, and wisest thing I know, that the soul exists, and that it is built entirely out of attentiveness. (p. 34)

—Mary Oliver from "Low Tide"
in *The Amicus Journal*

There are many ancient practices that can sensitize us to breath and its powers. The ancient meditative practice of Qigong, if performed with regularity, not only empowers one's breath but also serves to keep the balance of energies within the body. Body, breath, and energy are all intimately inter-related, and that Qigong, practiced regularly, balances body, mind, and breath into a naturally functioning, aware and organic whole.

The ancient Chinese practice of Qigong (pronounced *chee-gong*) has many different branches. I will present one particular practice, but all of the various practices are worth investigation by any musician who values breath and the awareness of breath. I have found that even after one session of this ancient meditative and energy practice, I feel energized and renewed. And I was amazed to find that the practices had much in common with my training as a conductor. In fact, the skill for acquiring "Qi" (or energy) through this practice has proved to be a valuable daily tool for me. Aside from the valuable energy aspects of the art, there are many additional health benefits.

A QIGONG PRIMER FOR MUSICIANS: CULTIVATING QI

There can be no doubt about the benefits of various meditative/physical studies and/or practices that allow body, mind, spirit, and breath to maintain contact with each other. Yoga practitioners sing the praises of its constant practice and integration into one's lifestyle. Tae Kwon Do practitioners tout its benefit to overall mental and spiritual health and its abilities to center oneself and one's energies. The practice of Alexander Technique has gained many musician practitioners because of the body awareness that it teaches. Many musicians stumble into the benefits of these practices after they encounter some type of "stress" and "tension" that, in turn, impacts their music making through their inability to breathe. I would like to present here a relatively new viewpoint on the use of the ancient Chinese healing practice of Qigong as such a vehicle for musicians.[2] Qigong seems to be one practice that can not only lead to a replenishment of musician "energy stores" but also stabilize the access of breath through acquisition and balancing of the energy of Qi in conjunction with breath.[3]

WHAT IS QIGONG?

In my opinion, this phenomenon (of Qigong) can be compared with the launching and receiving principle in radio, for it is a special "field" in objective reality. If only you know how to receive Qi with the corresponding specific means, you can receive Qi to obtain its curing effect. (p. 68)

—Wen Wei Qu
in Pan Gu Mystical Qigong

---

2   I was first introduced to this practice in Sedona, Arizona, at the MiiAmo Spa. After one class, I immediately felt the results of this relatively simple and direct approach taught by Paulette, who is on the staff of that spa. I was also impressed because many of its central principles were not only easily acquired in one class, but were directly in line with the principles I believe are centrally important to the art of conducting and breathing.

3   My first familiarity with the term of Qi (pronounced *Chee*) was in my acquaintance with a school of conducting pedagogy in Japan where there are a minimum number of gestures taught. All gestures are taught as movement toward or away from Qi. This Qi point is what has been referred to in the Western world as the *ictus*.

If there is one concept that comes up in all forms of Chinese medicine it is that of Qi, or vital energy. Qi is the very backbone of the Chinese healing arts. It refers to the energy of the universe that is channeled from nature and runs through all of us. To have Qi is to be alive, while to have none is to be dead.

Qigong also relies on the manipulation of this vital energy. This is done through "meridians," channels that pass through all the vital organs of the body. There are twelve of these meridians, which correspond to twelve organs. These meridians are interconnected, so that one runs into the other and passes through the body like an invisible river of energy. Anyone can learn simple exercises to manipulate his or her own Qi. This practice is known as *internal* Qigong. (p. xiii)

The root of the way of life, of birth and change, is Qi; the myriad things of heaven and earth all obey this law. Thus Qi in the periphery envelops heaven and earth. Qi in the interior activates them. The source wherefrom the sun, the moon and the stars derive their light, the thunder, rain, wind and cloud their being, the four seasons and the myriad things their birth, growth, gathering and storing; all this is brought about by Qi. Man's possession of life is completely dependent upon this Qi. (p. 284)

—Hong Liu
in *The Healing Art of Qigong*

Let me try to summarize both the practice of Qigong and its benefits to musicians and plainchant at the risk of over-simplifying the concepts of this practice.[4] Basically stated, the mind/body exercises as advocated by this specific practice of Qigong allows the body to function in parallel as a type of radio device. Through Qigong, we learn to use the body as a "receiver" of energy (or Qi) that is constantly around us. This energy is carried in atoms and particles energized by the sun and moon, which are available for our "collection." The exercises are the collection devices that allow us as musicians to "re-charge" and "re-focus" providing direct benefits upon our physical, mental, and spiritual health. Acquisition of Qi may be felt as vitality. At times, we can feel a certain magnetic or energy force between our hands.

---

4   I would encourage readers who are interested in acquiring the skills for this practice to find a practitioner in Qigong (available at www.Pangushengong.org) and to read and study the concise book by Wen Wei Ou, *Pan Gu Mystical Qigong.*

Acquiring Qi possesses both conscious action and super-conscious action. Again, at the risk of sounding very New Age, Qigong aims at achieving within oneself a certain balance and harmony of the energy that is *around* you and *within* you. The energy within you can only be replenished from sources that are external to you. Qigong provides you with a way of harvesting the energy that is omnipresent in the environment around you. The key to acquisition is a mind that is calm and a spirit that is open and loving. Finally, Qigong teaches body positions that maximize this energy acquisition. It has also been my experience that when these "energy centers" become re-balanced, the breath becomes deeper and more meaningful. As you perform the Qigong exercises, you will find that the primary awareness that is gained is an intimate awareness and connection to your breath.

Energy Flow and Breath in Qigong

One of the most valuable images necessary in the practice of Qigong is the concept of energy and its connection to breath. This image is especially valuable for not only conductors, but all musicians. When visualizing the flow of energy throughout the body, visualize that the energy (and breath) flows through the *entire* body like water. This flow is constant, and its speed is directly related to the amount of external energy that can be brought into the body. Stated another way, we must be in a constant state of awareness of our entire body in order for energy to flow throughout all parts of our body in this way. Unawareness leads to severe blockages in energy, which in turn will manifest itself in human interaction problems and musical issues. Qigong is another vehicle by which we as musicians can maintain a state of constant physical awareness. Physical awareness is the catalyst for spiritual awareness (to be discussed in the next section). The goal is for musicians to acquire the skills by which energy acquisition becomes habitual and the feeling of liquid energy flow within the body is both a constant and a norm for daily existence.

The Basic Qigong Exercise Sequence:
The Twenty-Six Repetitions

In this specific practice of Qigong, the following exercises are performed sequentially.[5] Slow and constant movement is the key to ample energy acquisition. Twenty-six repetitions are required for each movement. This number is based upon spiritual numerology. A verbal recitation at the beginning and end of the exercise sequence frames the entire repetition sequence.

A prerequisite to all of these exercises is a sense of core body alignment. An approach to core alignment can be found in *Learn Conducting Technique with the Swiss Exercise Ball* (GIA, 2004). In fact, the core alignment of one's body can be best achieved through awarenesses gathered from sitting on a Swiss exercise ball, as described in that text. Being organized like an apple around a core (where the core is one's pelvis) is central to vital energy flow through the body. Without organizing your body around its core, it will be difficult, if not impossible, to experience the free flow of energy throughout your body. At all times during these exercises, awareness of alignment and body core must be maintained through constant body awareness. The following diagram is a necessary image for this to happen during the execution of the Qigong exercises.

---

5   For readers desiring additional detail, two sources should be consulted. *Pan Gu Mystical Qigong* by Ou Wen Wei offers a detailed, step-by-step description of this approach to Qigong. I would also encourage readers to visit the website of the Pan Gu Shengong International Research Institute: www.pangushengong.org

BREATHING

Proper images for breathing should be employed at all times. Body Mapping, as demonstrated with the eight-handed breathing exercise, is central to this process. Throughout all the exercises, it is most important to remember that the air comes into the body in a wave-like motion from top to bottom. Exhalation also occurs in a wave-like motion from top to bottom.

For those interested in gaining a deeper understanding and, consequently, benefit from Qigong, it is widely believed that a practice unique to Qigong should be studied and mastered. This breathing technique attempts to wed breath with spirit. Obviously, such a technique would be beneficial to musicians.

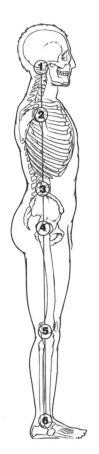

FIGURE 1.
THE SIX POINTS OF BALANCE
AND THE CORE OF THE BODY.

Before we enter this practice, I must emphasize one more thing. That is the entire embryonic breathing practice occurs through inner self-observation…That means "self-inner feeling." This feeling is the way your mind communicates with your physical body, Qi and Shen. This feeling can be shallow or profound, depending on how much you are able to calm down your mind and feel it. The level of feeling is unlimited, and normally follows the depth of your mind and awareness. Naturally, wrong feeling or mental perception can also lead you into fascination, illusion, and imagination. These false and unrealistic feelings can lead you to a state of emotional disturbance, and further away from the correct practice of Qi cultivation. (p. 323)

—Yang, Jwing-Ming
in *Qigong Meditation*

Tempo of the Exercises

All of the exercises must be performed in a slow tempo, somewhere between quarter = 42 and quarter = 60. The speed of the movement in the hands must be both constant and unvarying. It is the constant slow speed of the hand movements that allows you to both feel and gather energy from the atmosphere surrounding your hands. Maintaining a consistent speed is most important in the performance of the exercise sequence.

Starting Position and Recitation

This position is most important. The palms-up position of the hands allows for energy or Qi to enter the body and, in essence, recharge it. The belief is that energy enters the energy meridians of the body through the palms. Spend approximately two minutes in this position as you focus your thought on the breath, devoid of ego. To assist in getting ego out of the way, and beginning the proper flow of energy, many practitioners of Qigong encourage an out-loud recitation. This recitation, no matter its form, should include elements of giving, sharing, acquiring, and love. A sample of such a recitation is as follows:

> Take kindness and benevolence as basis;
> Take frankness and friendliness as bosom.
> Speak with reason; Treat with courtesy;
> Move with emotion; Act with result.[6]

---

6   Wen Wei Ou from title page *of Pan Gu Mystical Qigong* (Unique Publications, 2008).

LEFT SIDE MOTION

For this exercise, move to the position shown below where the hands are parallel on the left side of the body. The hands should be no more than sixteen inches apart. Move the hands in a slow and circular clockwise motion, with the lower hand following the motion of the upper hand, but slightly behind the upper hand. Perform one complete rotation every two seconds. Twenty-six complete cycles should be performed.

FIGURE 2. LEFT SIDE MOTION

MOTION TRANSFER FROM LEFT TO RIGHT

After the twenty-six rotations are completed, take both hands and move them to the center of the body, parallel with your navel. Transition the same position to the right side of the body. As you transition, the hand that was on the bottom is now on the top on the right side of the body.

FIGURE 3. MOTION TRANSFER FROM LEFT TO RIGHT

RIGHT SIDE MOTION

Perform the same circular motion with the left hand on top, and right following it. Perform one complete rotation every two seconds. Twenty-six complete cycles should be performed.

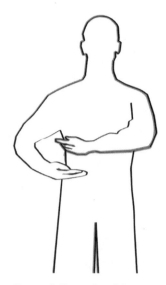

MIDDLE MOTION

After the motion has been completed on the right side of the body, turn your hands so they are parallel with the midline of your body, and rotate the hands, one following the other, for twenty-six forward rotations, with each rotation taking at least two seconds. The slower the rotations, the greater the benefit.

FIGURE 4. RIGHT SIDE MOTION

DRAWING OPEN MOTION

After you have completed the repetitions in middle motion, still your hands. Open your arms slowly while inhaling.

FIGURE 5: MIDDLE MOTION

FIGURE 6: DRAWING OPEN MOTION

DRAWING CLOSE MOTION

After exhaling and moving to the drawn open position, return to middle position while exhaling, arriving at a flower or "cupped" position of the hands.

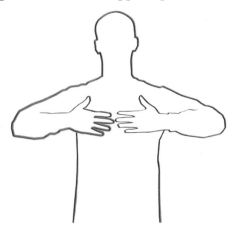

FIGURE 7: DRAWING CLOSE MOTION

FLOWER FOCUSING MOTION

After the drawing close motion, bring your hands into a cupped position, as if your hands are holding a flower. This hand position should mirror the position of your chin line and be approximately two to four inches below the chin. Stay in this position for approximately two minutes. If time permits, repeat the entire sequence again.

FIGURE 8: FLOWER MOTION (FOCUSING MOTION) AND RECITATION

CHAPTER 3
CHANT AND THE CLAIRVOYANCE OF BREATH

Tap into your silence. Listening and receiving…You are empty in a way so that the impulse has someplace to enter. Let the ear be your main organ.

—M. C. Richards in
The Fire Within

For a composition is, after all, an organism. It is a living, not a static thing. That is why it is capable of being seen in a different light and from different angles by various interpreters or even by the same interpreter at different times. Interpretation is, to a large extent, a matter of emphasis. Every piece has an essential quality which the interpretation must not betray. (p. 225)

—Aaron Copland
in *What to Listen for in Music*

At the macroscopic level, the brain—like the body—is a structure with a remarkable degree of bilateral symmetry. The mind, however, has but a single stream of consciousness, not two. (p. 294)

—Christof Koch
in *The Quest for Consciousness*

On the subject of air, teachers of breathing tell me they enjoy far more success with their students when they are very clear in their language, particularly when they distinguish air and breath. Air is a substance which occupies the planet along with us. Breath is a reflexive human movement that allows us to move air in and out of our bodies, and the air goes only into our lungs through a short passage.

Breathing is a movement which can be clearly (and deliciously) felt. Free breathing is beautiful to feel and beautiful to see. (p. 73)

—Barbara Conable
in *How to Learn the Alexander Technique*

What do you want to say? You've left a whole page of poetry but no place to take a breath. (p. 58)

—Bernard Greenhouse
in Diane Asseo Griliches,
Teaching Musicians

We are at liberty to be real, or to be unreal. We may be true or false, the choice is ours. We may now wear one mask and now another, and never, if we so desire, appear with our own true face. But we cannot make these choices with impunity. Causes have effects, and if we lie to ourselves and to others, then we cannot expect to find truth and reality whenever we happen to want them. If we have chosen the way of falsity we must not be surprised that truth eludes us when we finally come to need it. (p. 214)

—Thomas Merton
in Richard Todd,
The Thing Itself

Trust thyself. Every heart vibrates to that iron string. Envy is ignorance…Imitation is suicide. (p. 228)

—Ralph Waldo Emerson
in Richard Todd,
The Thing Itself

For all of us, there are moments of pristine clarity in our thought processes. These moments, for the most part, pass us by. They pass us by because we are not aware that they happen. They are short, quiet times that *coincide* with our inhalation process. The poet John Audelay in the twelfth century referred to such processes as moments that "bind blood to bone." Breath in those moments binds human emotion to expressive thought. This binding process is perhaps what this book is all about. An awareness of the power of this specific time in the chain of events characterized by the creative process within the artist's soul. It is a moment that is composed of quiet solitude, intense clarity of idea, and the human *will* for the breath to be the carrier of that idea.

If we allow and accept that there is this clairvoyant "opening," then we can feel a certain freedom to empower the breath with its message. I have heard it said by several teachers that musicians must "go deeper." Using this statement is confounding and eludes the real process involved within the performers. "Going deeper" is a separate process and a separate path, and that journey is one that must be taken separately. As William Sloan Coffin spoke of it, it is the "journey from the head to the heart." I have spent much time trying to inspire and articulate that journey in previous books.[7] "Going deeper" is a label for that intensely personal journey that every musician must ultimately take to empower the breath. This knowledge is not automatic, and in many ways it only becomes known at an intuitive level after one acknowledges that it does, indeed, exist. "Going deeper" must be known. Where one lives deep within oneself must also be known. Perhaps that is the most accurate definition of one's Center. That knowledge of self is acquired through an acknowledgment that it does, in fact, exist and that one has mined sufficiently within oneself where those things are. That deep belief that one has a message to relay through the composer's craft is also prerequisite to this breath empowerment.

---

7   These ideas can be found in *The Musician's Soul*, *The Musician's Spirit*, and *The Musician's Walk*, and in a certain way in *Toward Center*.

BEING AWARE OF THE MOMENT OF SILENCE

Psychologists tell us that when we are confronted with any decision we must make for either our living or our musicing, after processing ideas and thoughts, there is a silent nanosecond within our brain when a "decision" is made. For an artist, that nanosecond of silence is the moment at which the musical and human idea is clarified and becomes crystalline clear. For artists, that moment must correspond *with* the breath. But in many of us, the idea comes *after* the breath. Idea after breath deeply sabotages musical and human expression at every turn. In that moment when a nanosecond of silence is the by-product of thought, it is in *that* moment that we must bind that idea, that truth, that artistic honesty to our breath. In that moment, our breath becomes the messenger that informs our tone and all that we create in our world of sound. That moment of the binding of breath to idea must be sacred in our creative process. With every breath comes another "moment" to bind human message to the composer's score. This is a process of acknowledgment of the power of that nanosecond to inject truth and honest artistic expression into our music making. It is at the moment of inhalation that our truths about the music are powerfully bonded together. Once we begin to play, sing, or conduct an idea, we cannot do it as we are creating the musical line; the idea is birthed in the breath. Idea is created with breath, not in the process of creating sounds or influencing them through conducting gesture. Musical idea is forethought rather than afterthought. Breath carries the musical forethought, which is the truth and the idea that is conveyed through either text or notes.

Breath cannot escape one's body without an opinion.

—Nova Thomas
on *The Musician's Breath (DVD)*

Now the interesting thing about singing is when we have the need or the desire to make audible this thing that goes on forever. I promise you, technically, ALL you want to think about is inhaling. Just keep the feeling of drawing in the breath while you are singing, and make your thoughts audible. Three things I want you to know today. The first is your mantra for the rest of your life: Hear it; I mean hear it exactly how you want it to be heard in every aspect.

You hear THAT, you breathe into THAT, and you make THAT audible.

—Thomas Hampson
from a Masterclass at Westminster Choir
College, November 19, 2009
in James Jordan,
The Musician's Breath

You don't have to justify what is in that space before you speak.

—M. C. Richards
in *The Fire Within*

CHAPTER 4
WHAT DOES TRUSTING OTHERS SOUND LIKE?

Imagine how boring Jascha Heifetz would have been if he were only a wonderful technician. He is a great violinist because he goes beyond the notes. For a singer, this is even more important, because we have words as well as notes. We must do everything an instrumentalist does plus more. It is very serious and difficult work, and it is not done out of bravura or by willpower alone, but out of love, a devotion to what you adore. This is the strongest reason for anything. (p. 4)

—Maria Callas
in John Ardoin,
Callas at Juilliard The Master Classes

There is something from the other side (of that painting) that comes through…but then I thought from the other side of what. Not the other side of the paper…but something from the other side of the senses that comes through is the way I put it. That's the only way I could account for what I was being filled with.

—M. C. Richards
in *The Fire Within*

Rabbi Pinhas often cited the words: "A man's soul will teach him," and emphasized them by adding: "There is no man who is not constantly being taught by his soul."

One of his disciples asked: "If this is so, why don't men obey their souls?"

"The soul teaches constantly," Rabbi Pinhas explained, "but it never repeats." (p. 86)

—Martin Buber
in *The Way of Man: Ten Rungs*

When we allow the experience of chanting in a community to take root, honesty in sound is the by-product. In the quote above by M. C. Richards, she talks of seeing through the colors of the painting to what is beyond or behind the colors that meet our eyes. I am beginning to believe that I was indeed fortunate to have teachers who always taught me in some way to listen "into" the sound. A simple parallel analogy would be to ask yourself, can you hear human and emotional (and even spiritual) content in one's speaking voice? I think most of us would answer that we can if we choose to be listening in a way that allows us to hear "inside" the sound or beneath the surface of the grammar and the syntax of what is being spoken. In music, the ability to hear "below the surface" of the sound is a skill that both teachers and conductors must not only develop, but develop to a very high level. The miracle of chant is that its simplicity demands us to trust others. To trust others… it is that very simple concept that allows for the most honest voice in music to emerge.

All of my teachers forced me in many different ways to hear things that were beyond the pitches, rhythm, and textural clarity of the work at hand. Hearing what is human and expressive in a sound has always been at the forefront of any rehearsing or conducting that I do. But even after over thirty years as a conductor, I do not claim to fully understand what all this "inner listening" is comprised of. I do know, though, that if we want our ensembles to be expressive, somehow we must move ourselves to higher ground that moves musical sound from mundane and "clean" to a level that communicates, soul to soul, at a deep level.

QUALITIES OF THE CHANTED SOUND BENEATH THE SURFACE

The qualities of the "sound beneath the surface" can be labeled for purposes of this discussion as "honest" and "vulnerable." Sound can and does, if permitted, carry those deep messages within its sonorance. Resonances that are brilliant have brilliance because the human spirit provides the "stuff" into such sounds. I believe that vulnerability, fostered and engendered by trust, has a singularly unique color that can be heard. Because of single line chant, and that chat performed in ensemble, honest and vulnerable sound or a product of the entire group, not individuals.

Conductors and teachers must understand that sound must be allowed to have a life of its own—not to be restricted or confined to an acoustic box. To confine sound is to confine both soul and spirit. Sound restricted by technical confines places borders on human expressivity. Certainly, there are parameters that must be defined, but those parameters somehow must not also unknowingly or unwillingly restrict the sound of the spirit.

Vulnerability is a specific quality in musical sound. Musicians must want to hear it in music the same way they want to hear it in meaningful everyday conversation. Vulnerable sound is luminescent…deeply compelling, impassioned, roundly resonant, soul warming, and humanly vibrant. Musical sound thatched with vulnerability draws us into it; its seductive qualities draw our ears toward it. Vulnerable sound does not allow for mere monitoring; it draws us inward, profoundly inward.

Expectation and standards of expectation are everything in this somewhat mystical process. Conductors and teachers must set a standard by which they are deeply vigilant to hear those mystical qualities in musical sound. We must be careful that we become aware when we are seduced *only* by correct pitch, correct rhythm, correct articulation, correct vowel. Those are the aural representations of the color in a painting that M. C. Richards speaks of above. If we let down our standards, we set a lower expectation for our own inner listening sense, and certainly a lower standard for the ensemble that can and is perceived wordlessly by any ensemble. The lesson I have learned to hear at this deep level is that our ears can only be opened by vulnerability tempered with a great deal of love. The alchemy of those two elements is one of the most powerful antidotes for not only opening one's ears, but throwing open in a way the doors of one's spirit to not only listen but also to communicate the deepest aspects of human experience. We become handicapped, in a sense, by our own neurology. Sheer human will can bypass the default in all of us that allows us, as my teacher Elaine Brown used to say daily, "to hear, but not really listen."

> The left hemisphere is specialized not only for the actual production of speech sounds but for the imposition of syntactic structure on speech and for much of what is called semantics—comprehension of meaning. The right hemisphere, on the other hand, doesn't govern spoken words but seems to be concerned with more subtle aspects of language such as nuances of metaphor, allegory and ambiguity—skills that are inadequately emphasized in our elementary schools but that are vital for the advance of civilizations through poetry, myth and drama. We tend to call the left hemisphere the major or "dominant" hemisphere because it, like a chauvinist, does all the talking (and maybe much of the internal thinking as well), claiming to be the repository of humanity's highest attribute, language. Unfortunately, the mute right hemisphere can do nothing to protest. (p. 133)
>
> —V. S. Ramachandran
> in *Phantoms in the Brain*

While the quote above may delineate the neurological challenges of listening while chanting in a deeper way, it does not identify those things that may "close the door" to our own ability as artists to hear meaning and honesty in sound at a deeper level. The ability to listen at the deepest levels is intimately tied to our ability to be truly vulnerable "in public." This ability to "open oneself" is both an acquired skill and an acquired taste. Vulnerability in public can at first blush be deeply uncomfortable, and even frightening until vulnerability becomes your friend, a safe partner in the musicing process. Chant allows one to enter the sacred place within the safety of others.

CHAPTER 5
WHAT CHANT ALWAYS KNEW ABOUT MUSIC LEARNING

Perhaps the most important thing we can learn about the development of chant notation is that it was developed *after* the chant itself: the first singers conceived the chant; later they wrote it down. Gregorian chant was in the first instance not only sung without notation, it was also composed without notation...Acknowledging this—that a piece of chant could exist in completed form in the singer's mind without any notation—is the most important step in understanding early notation, and in understanding chant as well. One of greatest problems modern scholars have faced in trying to understand Gregorian chant and its notation has been in grasping how the original singers could *know* chant, how they could perceive it, learn it and remember it without notation. A principal solution to this problem is the realization that not only was it possible for chant singers to learn and know what they sang without notation, it was and is the basic way we learn any kind of music.
(p. 148)

—Richard L. Crocker
in An *Introduction to Gregorian Chant*

This is the phenomenon of the accentus (from *ad cantum*: "for the chant"); the accent, "the soul of the word and seed of musical art," governs a whole new musical creativity. For there exists a true dynamism in the Latin word: the word is an evolving melody. The accented syllable rises in pitch, and this is counterbalanced by the final syllable descending to a structural note. The other syllables are carried along by this movement: those preceding the accent are a preparation for the highest point; those following are a transition toward the ending. All this happens within the unity of a single rhythmic entity, that of the word. (p. 33)

—Dom Daniel Saulnier
in *Gregorian Chant*

The rule that governs all other rules is that, pure melody apart, chant is an intelligent declamation, with the rhythm of speech well phrased…. (p. 14)

—Chanoine Gontier
in *Institutions liturgiques, Vol. 1*

Certain basic elements of music cannot be therefore written down, or at least, if one does manage to express them more or less exactly in writing, they cannot be reproduced from the written page. The process of writing them down has rendered them sterile. (p. 27)

—A. Danielou
in *Semantique musicale, 1927*

The neume (pneuma) is like a symbol, a projection of the vocal inflexions [sic] upon the parchment. Its aim is mimesis, to draw a picture of the musical reality, and to place before the eyes a sign directly accessible to the imagination. (p. 127)

—Dom Daniel Saulier
in *Gregorian Chant*

The last fifty years in music education have taught us to consider and, in fact reconsider, how we learn music. We have examined the common practice of the sixteenth through twenty-first centuries to try to extract the DNA of what we do rather than analyzing the DNA itself. While pedagogy crafted from what we do is important and invaluable, it is also necessary to go beneath the surface to the essential bones of choral music: monophonic chant. The short story of the reality of chant is that it was born out of communities of people who wished to express themselves in song. Chant grew from a basic DNA of embellishments birthed from a reciting tone, with communities of people breathing together, listening, and moving musical sounds forward. No one would argue that those outcomes are what we yearn for as musicians, conductors, and artists. To return to chant seems almost too elusive, too simple to contain the pedagogical "teeth" we think we need to teach our choirs to be musical. But perhaps we believe that because we have taken our pedagogical journey too far away from the essential elements of what it means to sing together.

What Do We Know About Music Learning?

Examining what we do and how we do it has placed a much-needed microscope on music teaching over the past forty years. It has been my privilege to take an important part of that journey through my study and subsequent Ph.D. learning from Edwin Gordon. There is no doubt in my mind that what Dr. Gordon has developed via Music Learning Theory is essential for any musician, teacher, or conductor. Consider the questions his research and writings pose: How do we really learn music. How do we teach "listening" (audiation)? At the risk of oversimplifying Music Learning Theory, let me capsulate what I believe are the real "take-away" lessons from Dr. Gordon's lifetime of work on the subject.

1. **All Music learning must be based upon building audiational skills, not reading skills.** It is audiation—and only audiation—that can bring real meaning to notation. Audiation is the ability to hear music without it being physically present.

2. **Audiation of what is to come is birthed in the breath prior to what is sung or sounded.** To truly listen to others in the moment of inhalation should be at the very roots of any pedagogy.

3. **We learn *harmonically*, not *melodically*.** Music literacy and the ability to read and perform music is based on our ability to make relationships between individual notes. We organize music *not* by interval, but rather by the implied chord structures that tones in relationship inhabit: e.g., Do–Mi–So are all notes comprising a tonic chord; Sol–Ti–Re–Fa are all notes that form the V7 harmonic unit. Chords in music are similar to words in language. In language, it is letters that form words with meaning. The same is true for music.

4. **Rhythm can only be realized when it is born out of consistent tempo.** For rhythm to have meaning it must have, at its root, a consistent tempo. Expressivity is born out of "communal" tempo felt and audiated by all.

5. **Singing together and playing together establishes an entrainment among and between musicians.** While Gordon's work did deal extensively with consistent tempo and the need for its establishment, it is my viewpoint that entrainment, a deeply perceptual act explained by physics, is what causes people to sing and play together in a consistent tempo.

6. **Intonation is a marriage of acoustic, listening, and honesty.** The ability to hear others, to sense others, and to make oneself "less so that others become more" is also essential for shaping a phrase.

7. **Phrases cannot be legislated; they must be a product of the natural behavior of sounds within a scale or mode and the inherent shapes implied by the tones.** To play with great "musicianship" is certainly a goal that we all share as teachers and conductors. Even though it is easier to use rehearsal devices to "show" an ensemble "how" to move sound forward, it is not a substitute for *awareness* of how the sound actually moves forward when a group of people respond in the moment to each other.

8. **In teaching music literacy, we should teach not only major and minor modalities, but all of the modes.** Modes are better able to teach phrase shape because they avoid cadential structures, or rather scale degrees that can mis-shape the natural ascent and descent of the musical line.

9. **Intonation is always a direct result of honest expression rather than theoretical manipulation of pitch.**

10. **Ear should always come before eye.** Meaning should be brought to notation from audiation rather than from its visual representation on the page.

11. **Musical skill is best developed when pitch is developed devoid of a rhythm structure, and vice versa.** One of the research developments in music learning the past forty years has proven that musicians learn best when pitch and intonation are learned devoid of a consistent tempo and that rhythm is more efficiently learned devoid of pitch. In plainchant, this cardinal rule of music learning is always observed. The audiation of pitch and the audiation of rhythm are complex neurological activities. When they are co-mingled, the research has shown that music learning is slowed, if not totally impeded, by the confusion of the two hierarchies of music.[8] Plainchant allows us to focus on the pitch and mode components of chant because of the flexibility of the rhythm—in essence, a free flow rhythm defined with a narrow parameter of tempo, but almost never in a rhythmically rigid and consistent tempo.

In studying Music Learning Theory and using it in my teaching for over thirty years, and also for those of you reading this book who have made decisions about teaching music literacy, I am sure you will agree with most, if not all, of the above statements. The irony of all of the above statements is that *all* of those principles are inherent in chant! In many ways, chant teaches the skills that we desperately need as musicians in a very direct and honest way. Perhaps the most important aspect of this book is its advocacy of re-establishing that notation should only be a representational system that is a sign for things already heard and experienced. The absence of accidentals, the use of modes, the lack of major and minor "modern" tonalities all grow musicianship with those who engage chant. Rhythm becomes an organic experience that is both felt and heard. Intonation inhabits the realm of harmonic functionality rather than a melodic function. Listening becomes multi-dimensional.

---

8   One of the most startling research discoveries for music education happened during the analysis of data in the development of *Primary Measures of Music Audiation* by Edwin Gordon. The data concerning the item analysis for individual items pointed to both higher validity and reliability when students were asked to discriminate pitch separate from rhythm, and vice versa. While that test points to students in the stage of developmental music aptitude before age nine, this author has experienced that students after that age through adulthood benefit from the separation of pitch and rhythm when learning a piece of music in rehearsal.

This book is an attempt to make us all realize that our pedagogical tools have been present all along. Listening, breathing, shaping, and feeling the community that singing together breeds are all present in chant. Finishing phrase endings becomes a communal event that requires a kind of "letting go" and relaxation. And most important, musical phrasing becomes a shaping of sound that is a broad event, that plots a beautiful trajectory of line—of ascent and descent. The very simplicity of chant allows us to develop a simple, direct, and honest way of expressing, through sound, the text. Through singing chant, we allow our musicianship to begin in that place where honesty and community abide—listening to each other and sensing the breath of a *community* of people. While chant teaches us many musical sensitivities, it is the human things that are taught to us through singing a single line that build both an ensemble's musicianship and the sense of what it is to sing and play together. To be part of something larger than oneself is, perhaps, one of the largest lessons of chant. Chant has pointed the way for several hundred years. Hopefully this book will redirect our attention to making our doing and teaching right at a very basic level.

CHAPTER 6
UNDERSTANDING "RESONANT RHYTHM" WITHIN PLAINSONG

But no, rhythm is not a mere question of intensity. It is a question of *movement*—of ordered movement; it is the grouping of sounds into a synthesis. In general, rhythm is essentially a synthesis. Its work is to withdraw each sound from its pure individuality and blend all into one large movement. This is done by a series of units, successively bigger and more comprehensive, the lesser enshrined in the greater, combining and reaching their mutual completion in one united whole. (p. 10)

—Joseph Gajard
in *The Rhythm of Plainsong*

This book advocates the use of chant as a means of building literacy and musicianship. It is easy, after some thought, to envision the reasons why chant could be a vehicle for teaching elements of pitch and phrasing. But we could ask: How can chant enrich the rhythm skills of singers when the notation itself is devoid of an organized system of rhythm notation?

I am advocating a look at building rhythm skills from another perspective. I have written much in the past twenty-five years concerning rhythm pedagogy. The chapter that follows details my research about the phenomenon of entrainment as a way of establishing consistent tempo. The crux of the matter in rhythm pedagogy has always been the challenge of teachers to establish consistent tempo. Without consistent tempo, there can be no decisive divisions of beats from a larger pulse that defines our modern methods of rhythm notation. But perhaps the fallacy here for all of us is that we have worried about getting to the understanding of notated rhythm before the core of our rhythm "sense" has been established. If we have the courage to take "another way in" to the teaching of rhythm, perhaps we will not only unlock the secrets that rhythm contains but also lead to a new level of musicianship for our ensembles. We have always talked about teaching rhythm from the "inside out," but do we really know what that is? Or better yet, do we really believe that there is a sense, a feeling, that is at the very core of rhythm performance and that connects us to ourselves in a fully human way?

None of us would argue that the performance of rhythm involves "feelings." I believe all of us would also agree that the performance of rhythm involves to one degree or another a feeling of a shifting of weight that creates the feeling of a pulse. While this may well be true, that concept and all those related to it may have been our Achilles heel all these years as we struggle to find efficient pedagogies for the teaching and feeling of rhythm. Perhaps we have been too worried about teaching the organization of rhythm rather than exposing our ensembles first to the larger perceptual experience that we call rhythm.

If we consider the following quote by Dom Joseph Gajard, and if we are open to its premise, then we can begin to understand why plainchant is perhaps the most organic and sensible way to understand rhythm from a perceptual point of view rather than a reading/mathematical division point of view.

This leads us to an interesting point. Because of the essential unity of the living being, there is a close, indeed, an absolute connection between vocal rhythm and that vital rhythm, which shows itself in local movement. Personally I am of the opinion that resonant musical rhythm is nothing more than the projection into order of sound of that vital movement which we all have within us. As long as you are unable to associate musical rhythm with your own vital rhythm, there is something wanting. Musical rhythm is only good in the measure in which it makes you feel your own rhythm. "By rhythm alone," M. Combarieu truthfully says, "resonant matter takes a form. It is rhythm which makes an organism, and an ordered and intelligible whole; so that the mind of the hearer, instead of vaguely hither and thither, rejoices in itself, as though its own harmony had been revealed to it." (p. 14)

—Joseph Gajard
in *The Rhythm of Plainsong*

I found the above quote shocking, illuminating, yet a bit intimidating. Frankly, it is easier to teach rhythm from the standpoint of dividing the "large beat" or macro beat into either two or three parts. It is much more difficult to commit first to teaching an awareness of rhythm through the rhythmic dynamic that exists when musicians engage in chant as a community. Perhaps the problem with our pedagogy is that, ultimately, we rely on the individual to "figure out" rhythm alone or in a solo context. While we may be able to intellectualize the dividing and parsing of a beat, we really can't explain what it means to have rhythm come from a place deep inside us that is felt alongside others. The statement above that "resonant matter takes form" could be considered a new definition of the foundations of rhythm learning and performance. As teachers and conductors, we must trust—and more importantly believe—that this is happening as a result of a plainchant experience. We also have to believe that this foundational rhythm sense is developed through a sensitivity toward the rise and fall of a single musical line. Now if we further alter our pedagogical paradigm to look at the larger perceptual issues involving rhythm, we can begin to make sense of the effect that plainchant has upon the rhythm awareness of any ensemble.

In general, rhythm is essentially a synthesis. Its work is to withdraw each sound from its pure individuality and blend all into one large movement. This is done by a series of units, successively bigger and more comprehensive, the lesser enshrined in the greater, combining and reaching their mutual completion in one united whole. (p. 10)[9]

—Joseph Gajard
in *The Rhythm of Plainsong*

If we can separate ourselves from the way we have been taught to teach rhythm and instead examine the process by which we experience rhythm, our teaching paradigm may begin to morph. Chant asks us to rely first on listening within a community of people and being aware of the internal "combustion" that is created when texts, tune, and dynamic shapes come into play. A kinesthetic rhythm sense, the keystone of rhythm learning, is best acquired through a sonic world that involves others and immediately responds to the "physics" that is inherent in the rise and fall of a musical line. For those who have tried to analyze the effects of chant upon rhythm, this concept of "resonant matter taking form" seems to reveal itself through communal chant.

Personally, I am of the opinion that resonant musical rhythm is nothing more than the projection in the order of sound of that vital movement which we all have within us. As long as you are unable to associate musical rhythm with your own vital rhythm, there is something wanting. (p. 14)

—Joseph Gajard
in *The Rhythm of Plainsong*

---

9   Throughout all of his writing concerning Music Learning Theory, Edwin Gordon has advocated that teachers realize the value of teaching small units or rhythm patterns as a step in acquiring rhythm literacy.

And, most importantly, consider:

> In a word, rhythm is the **relation** which is established between two elements, a rise and a fall, fusing them together in the unity of a single movement. Or, more exactly still, rhythm is the unity of movement brought about by the relation established between two elements, a rise and a fall. (p. 15)

> —Joseph Gajard
> in *The Rhythm of Plainsong*

> The causality principle asserts that the connection between cause and effect is a necessary one. The synchronicity principle asserts that the terms of a meaningful coincidence are connected by simultaneity and meaning. (p. 95)

> —C. G. Jung
> in *Synchronicity*

So what plainchant does for an ensemble is that it permits us to experience the large picture before the small. We learn phrasing before we acquire the intricacies of modern rhythm notation that attempts to notate the un-notatable! Plainchant allows us to experience phrase shape and experience consistent tempo as a by-product of listening and singing together, which more powerfully affects not only our musicianship but also ultimate understanding of rhythm. Chant also frees us from the visual dogma that notation commands. Reading notation before experiencing this *resonant rhythm* of plainchant robs us of the context of rise and fall, ebb and flow, and the internal sense of pulse each of us carries within us. As teachers and conductors, it is perhaps more pedagogically beneficial to build our rhythm house first from a communal sense of harnessed kinetic energy rather than force some type of rhythm sense onto notation. Sound before sign has always served music educators well. Feeling rise and fall, and trusting that that innate ability is within each of us, is perhaps a better pedagogical starting block.

"In" a Meter versus "On" a Meter

Understanding the difference between "in" and "on" regarding meter can further define the rhythmic flexibility contained in plainsong. "In" a meter can be defined as the performance of rhythm with exact subdivisional units that are always equal and exactly proportionate because they are performed over the top of a somewhat rigid consistent tempo. "On" a meter is meant to describe music performance that has a forward-moving communal pulse, but not necessary always in the same tempo. To be "on" a meter, the tempo of a plainchant must be rooted deep within each musician, and it is mediated, balanced, and sensed through listening and kinesthetic feeling. Plainchant should never be "in" a meter, but should live "on" a flexible pulse that is always initiated by breath energy.[10] Animation of the breath sets both the spirit and the parameters of tempo of the plainchant that follows.

This level of musicianship and phrasing can readily be developed within any choral ensemble with a few simple rules that govern the initiation of any plainchant phrase. When we master this in plainchant, it becomes a relatively easier matter to incorporate the same procedure in the singing of performance literature.

Initiating and Teaching Communal Breathing Using Plainchant

1. Always energize the breath.
2. Know the ascent and descent of the musical phrase; it is this knowledge of phrase trajectory that, in turn, informs the breath and gives it actual musical content—a sort of phrasal uploading.
3. Do not begin any chant until all singers perceive a calm in the room.
4. The group should strive to breathe together, ideally without a conductor. Singers should develop skill to the point where they intimately sense the breath of others.

---

10   One cannot overemphasize the importance of inspirited, energized, and actualized breath in the performance of chant. The initial tempo combined with the energy of the breath sets up the forward movement of the chant. This practice of "soul feeling" the breath, the "animation" of the breath is dealt with in detail in the book, *The Musician's Breath* (GIA, 2011).

CHAPTER 7
UNDERSTANDING ENTRAINMENT INHERENT IN CHANTING

One thought only: rhythmic problems are not primarily problems of reading—for us. We repeat things often enough so that it should be difficult for a sightless person to make more than a few mistakes. The primary problem is that of *feeling*. Now, that is a fairly indeterminate "term," but what I'm trying to say is that the "sense" of rhythm is a mighty complex thing: physical, physiological, psychological, visceral, etceteractual; and our problem as a group is not that of visual identification—two quarter notes equal one half note—but that of getting people to *experience* two quarter notes simultaneously physically, physiologically, psychologically, viscerally and etceteractually. We turn the old grade school apology, "I know what it is, but I can't put it into words," all the way around. We can put rhythm into words—symbols—but we have no idea what it is. (p. 65)

—Robert Shaw
in *The Robert Shaw Reader*

The gait of man and beast, the flight of birds, the circulation of the blood, and the breathing process are rhythmicized. (p. 93)

—Wilhelm Ehmann
in *Choral Directing*

All life consists of rhythmic processes. From the simple pulsations
of a single-cell organism to the rising and falling of our breath, life is
filled with rhythm. This rhythm is also called "periodicity," meaning
that the activity of something falls in cycles. Much of life is directed
by the external rhythms of nature. For example, the earth spins on
its axis and rotates around the sun, and around our moon orbits the
earth. We attune ourselves to the cycles of the sun and the moon,
following the different rhythms they create. With day and night,
different behavior is created; we usually get up with daylight and go
to sleep at night. When our light-dark cycle is disturbed, as when we
take a long jet flight, our ability to function in the new environment is
affected for a day or two. We call this "jet lag." Different behavior due
to rhythm also occurs for the different seasons of the year and the
response of nature to this. Not only our sleep patterns, but our eating
patterns, digestive patterns, even our harvesting and mating patterns
are affected by the rhythms of these cycles.

—Jonathan Goldman
from Sonic Entrainment website:
www.healingsounds.com/sonic-entrainment

R hythm pedagogy has dealt by and large with surface approaches to teaching rhythm. For many years, pedagogies reflected approaches to using movement to reinforce kinesthesia or body feelings associated with rhythm. The work of Dalcroze made great inroads toward a deeper understanding of the rhythm learning/kinesthesia process. However, if we spend some time examining the roots of our rhythm experience, we discover that many more "basic" kinesthetic readinesses must be established before rhythm can be learned in a musically meaningful and expressive way. Jazz musicians have always talked about being in "a groove." If we consider what organically constitutes "a groove," a clarity about teaching all of the components of rhythm and their interactions becomes clear. There is an organic readiness that must be in place before rhythms can be experienced, audiated, and then processed through the innate kinesthesia of the rhythm being performed.

Much has been said about becoming "expressive" with rhythm. The intent of this book is to put forth a pedagogy by which this expressivity can be taught and understood by performers. Music ensembles, because of their numbers, provide a unique pedagogical opening for conductors and teachers. The key to rhythm learning involves two important factors: (1) establishing rhythm entrainment and (2) teaching musicians rhythm that grows out of harmonic progression. This book proposes that "expressivity" in rhythm is best taught in union with harmonic progression. Musicians need to be taught to infer the messages contained within harmonic rhythm and then learn rhythm phrasing ideas that are an outgrowth of those harmonic structures and a response by the performers of engaging the harmonic motion of any piece to arrive at "expressive" rhythm.

Gaining an Understanding of Entrainment

Entrainment can be thought of as sympathetic resonance between bodies. All things (including human beings) have resonances that can be set in motion when they share similar frequencies or are allowed to accept the vibrating frequency of a larger group of objects or persons. In 1665, Dutch physicist Christian Huygens discovered that if you have several pendulum clocks with different-length pendulums, after a period of time, no matter their size, the clocks would all synchronize with each other.

Entrainment also is interactive. The power of entrainment is that you can change the natural oscillatory patterns of one object (musician) and replace them with another (as initiated by a metronome). When one is aware of entrainment, one can find its effects everywhere. The connections may be as simple as a conversation between two people becoming in the same "tempo" to a great public speaker and the response of a crowd being in the same tempo (e.g., the Martin Luther King "I Have a Dream" speech). In medicine, there has been research concerning the effects of sound entrainment upon entrainment of both hemispheres of the brain. While the research has been somewhat limited, its conclusions point strongly to the profound and direct influence of entrainment upon our body rhythms and the energy that courses throughout us.

Sound entrainment has been used in Tibetan mediation practice for centuries. Jeff Strong and The Rhythm Entrainment Institute maintains that rhythm patterns can be categorized for specific therapeutic results (calming, dyslexia, autism). His discussions and experimental data form a compelling case as to the power of entrainment.

Entrainment Must Be Established

No matter the medium employed, establishing entrainment is central to all long-term rhythm understanding. Equalization of the body's energy allows for musicians to function within a consistent energy flow so rhythms can be perceived, audiated, and performed with meaning. A short period of time where musicians listen and absorb sound moving in a consistent manner is essential for them to organize, assimilate, audiate, and perform rhythm. Entrainment, while at first glance seems to be a simple, almost too-obvious component of the rhythm experience, it is the foundation for all rhythm learning and understanding. Entrainment also influences rhythmic breathing, which has profound effects on the rhythms that grow out of breath. Breathing within musicians affects the tempo, color, emotional intent, and dynamic of the music that is to follow. Entrainment also reflects the ebb and flow of the harmonic rhythm that underlies any piece of music. Aural entrainment is a powerful tool that allows for other levels of rhythm learning to take place in a natural way.

CHAPTER 8
LISTENING

Music like this, music about listening, is relatively rare because it is a self-conscious disclosure of the condition of possibility for listening unselfconsciously. (p. 159)

Listening is a kind of utterance by which utterance is received. (p. 157)

—Lawrence Kramer
in *Expression and Truth*

T. S. Eliot speaks of "music heard so deeply that it isn't heard at all, but you are the music while the music lasts." And he sees in this experience an aspect of "the moment in and out of time." When we learn to combine the two and live "in and out of time," we turn the polarity between time and now, between instant and ecstasy, into a creative tension. This inner gesture allows us to live full and creative lives.

Involvement with chant instills in us that inner gesture of listening and response, which then apply to any activity in the course of the day. (p. 11)

—David Steindl-Rast
in *Music of Silence*

As conductors and teachers we often admonish our groups to "Listen! Listen!" we say, "for details of the harmonic and melodic elements of music must be accurate. Voices must be clear, beautiful, and well balanced."

Less often do conductors remember to say, "Listen! Listen! to the composer of the musical details, and to the author of the text. Listen to the spirit of these men and the ideas reflected in their music."

There is another kind of listening which the conductor-teacher should encourage in his singers, but seldom does. He rarely says, "Listen! Listen to that which is best in yourselves." Why does he not provide for this ultimate "in-listening"? It must be either that he has not discovered the source of what brings out the best in himself, or that he is driven by the usual economic and schedule pressures involved in building a "successful" choir, and is afraid to make provision for listening in the deepest sense of the word.

There are two kinds of listening which become increasingly difficult to experience in the mad rush of everyday living. The first has to do with knowing how to be alone, how to listen long enough and carefully enough to our own thoughts, until we father a series of tappings of our own resources. The second has to do with learning to listen to others, not just accommodatingly and passively, but to *listen* to others.

Here and there, like a cry in the night, a thinking man is heard to say: "Stop right where you are and think! Listen while there is yet time." For the most part, this advice goes unheeded. (pp. 86–87)

—Elaine Brown
in *Lighting a Candle*

I am not sure I understand all of the things that contribute to one's ability to listen, especially in chanting. The initial pedagogical challenge for all musicians is that many musicians *hear* but do not *listen*. On first blush, I may be accused of playing with semantics. Despite the frequent inadequacies of the English language, the differences between hearing and listening should be noted. What I am quite certain about is that chant compels us to listen, not just hear. Chant has re-sharpened and re-defined my pedagogical process regarding how to guide musicians to listen. Why?

Because if we are engaged in listening, we seemingly become immersed in, almost surrounded by, sound that makes its way into every part of our being. Listening is deeply inward, and it demands a type of centeredness and internal openness to sound, and to others, that is difficult to discover.

Hearing

When we merely "hear," we monitor sound from an external vantage point. When we "hear" a musician, we seem to detach and distance ourselves from sound. When we merely hear sound around a musician, it is recognized as a detached event, and the content of what is being played or sung is never engaged. For the most part, hearing is the auditory skill we use and employ in everyday life. Hearing in everyday life is selective in that we hear everything, but we screen what we choose to process and understand. For most musicians, a weakness in rehearsal pedagogy is that the warm-up process does not transform passive hearing to active and depthful listening. Hearing also runs the risk of not recognizing many components of either sung or played sound. In the end, hearing is not audiation. By using the term "audiation," I am labeling a process that is at the core of how we learn music. As Edwin Gordon has written many times, we should "teach audiation." Teaching our musicians to audiate should be the overriding objective in all that we do.

The Experience of Listening

I have thought long and hard about what the experience of listening really is. Because it is a total experience, it perhaps can be described through analogy. On a recent trip to Great Britain, James Whitbourn took me to a small country church, All Saints Church in Tudeley. This small, unassuming country church sits in the midst of a very small village and beautiful rolling British countryside.

James Whitbourn related the story that a benefactor, a member of the church congregation, wanted to memorialize his daughter who had died in a tragic drowning accident. He contacted Marc Chagall and asked him to accept a commission for a stained glass window to be installed above the main altar. Chagall came to install the window and felt that the other smaller windows, made of clear leaded glass, didn't cast the right light for the rest of the church, so he asked if he could do all of the other windows in this small country church. The installation of all of the windows was completed in 1986 just before Chagall's death.

Upon entering the small church from the side/rear entrance, one's senses are immediately drawn to the incredible window over the main altar. Its radiance, color, and intensity take you by surprise. You are drawn to the window. Your sight becomes the most important sense in that very moment. The room surrounds you with a blue luminescence that is warm and enfolding. And the color wash in the room places you in another place, another world. All that matters to your senses are the colors as your eyes move from one window to another. You are truly surrounded by "beauty," and that beauty causes a deep inward calm and deepened awareness. All that seems to matter is to experience the color and the beauty of the place. Unlike viewing a singular work of art, the art filters the light and uses it to create a visual and visceral experience. And, remarkably, you remain in its grasp for the full time you are in the space of that church.

Experiencing the Tudeley windows equaled (but in a slightly different way) my experience many years ago viewing the windows of Chartres Cathedral in France. Both sets of windows use enormous amounts of blue in the glass. Both sets of windows seem to filter the light in such a way as to focus and disperse it. You become overwhelmed trying to take in all that the windows have to offer.

But seeing the Tudeley Church with Chagall's masterpieces at every turn is a slightly different experience in a very important way. Because of the smallness of the church, with the exception of the main window, all of the windows are at eye level. You can choose to view the window from afar or walk right up to the window, almost like a human microscope. The windows provide another total experience when up close. When you are up close, you not only see the colors but you can also see the prints of Chagall's hand in the color! You see slight, beautiful variations of the color in the same pane of glass...a world within a world. The fine details deepen and enrich what already is a moving experience from afar.

Hearing is like the experience of viewing the windows from afar. You become aware of the overall effect, but not until you really see, just not look, by viewing the windows close up are you drawn into another, deeper experience. Listening, for musicians, should be the same experience as viewing those windows close up. The colors in each window perhaps could represent all the people in the community that is known as the ensemble. The close-up viewing could parallel the experience of listening deeply and inwardly to sound. For me, chant is a remarkably parallel experience to viewing those windows. Chagall and the sound of monophonic chant are remarkably similar experiences if you allow yourself to not only be surrounded by the sound in the community of others but also listen so closely that you hear every minute detail of both sound and expression.

As musicians, we believe that we "listen" to the music we make. Truth be told, we mostly monitor from afar, being content with *hearing* sound from a distance, but not really listening. To listen, we must *want* to listen, which requires us to open ourselves in such a way that allows us to listen. We must deeply want to listen to others and, in an ensemble, become part of something larger than ourselves. It is listening deeply embedded within the community of others that allows us to take the journey that plainchant affords. James Whitbourn remarked as we left that little church, "Isn't it astounding how those windows transform that small space into a deeply meaningful aesthetic experience?" For musicians, plainchant can do the same thing. The difference is that we must want to listen deeply to hear what miracles plainchant contains. Passive hearing will never allow chant to work its magic. There must be a desire for community, a desire to listen as one, and a desire to be part of a larger community but still in a relationship with everyone in the room. I often refer to the writings of Martin Buber, especially in his book *I and Thou*. Buber's overriding premise is that "community is where community happens." Within that community, it is deeply important that individuals are connected to each other in a one-to-one relationship with each other. Meaningful and life-altering listening can only be experienced when both of these principles are in place. The miracle of what we experience with chant is that through the monophony of chant, a stronger deepening can be realized because of what plainchant calls upon us to do—to be in communion with others with sound as the yeasting agent. For musicians, there is no greater lesson or skill to be learned. Our ears must perform daily the miracle of Marc Chagall's windows and draw us into what it means to be and to sing together. While Chagall's windows create a sacred space in that Tudeley church imbued with deep beauty, we must not forget that as musicians it is our responsibility to create a sacred space for profound listening to sound and each other. We can create a sacred space for music only by listening deeply to others and to ourselves in a kind of sonic communion with self and sound. An awareness of others, coupled in the same moment with a deep awareness of sound in all its dimensions (sonic and spiritual), is the very definition of listening. When all of that occurs, the music we sing with each other gains a voice of deep and compelling honesty—as compelling as Chagall's windows.

In the end, there is simply no better vehicle for teaching those lessons than plainchant. "When our being is right, the doing takes care of itself," Elaine Brown always used to say to her students. When your being is right, the "doing" of listening *will* take care of itself. And it is plainchant that can give you the tools to "make your being right."

AN ARCHITECTURAL INTERVENTION AND AFTERTHOUGHT

As an addendum to the above discussion, I must add once again that my "discoveries" about plainchant were realized during the 2013 Choral Institute at Oxford, which was held at St. Stephen's House, one of the permanent halls of Oxford University. St. Stephen's occupies the architectural wonders of George Frederick Bodeley. Bodeley was perhaps the greatest architect of the nineteenth-century Anglican tradition. In particular, Bodeley wanted to "get it right" so to speak designing the entire building, especially the smaller Chapel and the larger St. John the Evangelist Church. That church was designed for chant. So in retrospect, it should be no surprise that, like the Chagall windows, the very sound of plainchant in both of those rooms allowed us to listen as a community and as individuals, which chant requires of us. Both rooms created a special resonance that not only gave plainchant a voice but also drew us all into listening.

CHAPTER 9
GENERAL MUSICAL/PERFORMANCE/ TEACHING PRINCIPLES

For many people today the notion of "free" or speech rhythm in music is difficult. We are so used to harnessing words into beats that it's hard to undo that bond. But we must make the attempt because only then can the subtle beauties of the single-line melody be released. When we get it right, when the words are enhanced by the curling melodic phrases, it is an unparalleled path to contemplation, to musical ecstasy. One must listen so completely to other singers, one must so submerge the ego in these rigorous demands, so focus on the sound and the meaning of the text, that all else disappears. Because there is no hurry, we can relax. Because the voice is never pushed, we can sing beautifully. Because we are so completely immersed in the text, its meaning is revealed to us in full glory. This music is the perfect antidote to the tension, hurry, and loudness of our times. (pp. 88–89)

—Alice Parker
in *The Anatomy of Melody*

Calling and responding belong to the very essence of the music. Chant is not a solo performance, it's a choir performance. And it's the whole community that chants, not specialized singers. What matters is not the singer but the song, the self-transcending responsiveness that chant demands. (p. 6)

—David Steindl-Rast
in *Music of Silence*

On St. Benedict's Rule:

One aspect of the Rule is stability; that means perseverance, or even stubbornness. Once you've started a job, do it. Don't let your energy be deflected by other conflicting interests. An important part of the tradition is contained in the first word of the Rule: "Listen!" Listen to the sounds of creation: the wind, the trees, the animals, the people. Another concept that is important to me in the Rule is humility, humble, human, humus, the earth. (pp. 13–14)

—Mark W. McGinnis
in *The Wisdom of the Benedictine Elders*

How we experience ourselves is reflected in the way we can approach and experience other people: we cannot know other people better than we know our own selves; we cannot trust other people more than we trust our own selves. (p. xxii)

—Stephanie Dowrick
in *Intimacy and Solitude*

A marvelous and special art lies hidden in unison singing, and most of our choirs today would fail if they were tested on their ability to sing monadic music. Unison singing is a true test of a choir's real ability. It serves as a good test of the choir's singing skill and artistry, and any time and effort spent in this area will improve multi-voiced singing. (p. 151)

—Wilhelm Ehmann
in *Choral Directing*

In speaking of his philosophy of music, Tabuteau often referred to the "laws of nature." To explain his concept of the "life" of the notes and of the "up and down impulses," he used illustrations ranging from the movement of the earth around the sun to the motion involved in our own normal respiration or the way one must lift the foot before being able to put it down. (p. x)

—Laila Storch
in *Marcel Tabuteau*

Music is life, a living art. It is governed by natural laws as are all living things. Music should not work contrary to nature but in accordance with it and with all those forces that have a continuous effect upon us. As a living being must breathe, so must music. It must inhale as well as exhale. Music can be described as a combination of inhalations and exhalations; as life is in continuous movement, so must it be with music. There is constant motion all around us and within us. Music being life must have this continuous movement, pulse, and direction to remain alive. (p. 534)

—Marc Mostovoy
in Laila Storch, *Marcel Tabuteau*

When asked, most music teachers and those involved with teaching music performance at some level would agree that teaching musicians and ensembles to "be musical" is an over-riding objective. We teach phrase direction through kinesthetic involvement. We teach shaping of line through text emphasis and direction. Most often, these techniques allude to some sort of mystical method that points the way to "being musical." And those techniques increase a musician's awareness about how sounds move forward and are shaped. The problem facing all of us as conductors and teachers is that such techniques grow phrasing from the "outside in."

Attempts to explain the art of musical phrasing and the artistry connected with it have birthed many pedagogical approaches. Dalcroze, through Eurythmics, attempted to embody phrase direction through kinesthetic understandings (and cognitive understandings) of the constant interaction of time, space, and weight. At the turn of the century, Marcel Tabuteau, renowned oboe teacher at the Curtis Institute, codified what to this day is probably the most elegant way of describing the parameters and execution of artistic musical phrasing. Those principles were elegantly summarized in the 1950s by James Thurmond in his book entitled *Note Grouping*. The clarity and far-reaching principles in that book were advanced through the teaching and performances of both Robert Shaw and Weston Noble.

But as with any pedagogical approach, we reach a point where the mechanics of any system must yield a spontaneous result without constant pedagogical reminder and reinforcement. Stated another way, we hope that somehow our teaching will grab hold and allow our students to be "musical" on their own—that, in some way, they may develop an intuition about phrasing that is organic, natural, and honest.

Intuitive phrasing, if it is to have any relevance, must develop out of a sense of listening to others, sublimating oneself to a larger dynamic and a keen sensitivity about what is happening around oneself in an ensemble. Breathing, listening, sensing, and even a bit of sacredness for sound must be present for musical ideas to take hold.

What has amazed me the past year using chant as a "warm-up" in every rehearsal is that chant does begin the process from the "inside out." Performed, in most cases without a conductor, phrasing grows from the intuition of the group (not from any force or controlled influence that compels the sound to move forward, or rather makes it move forward). The miracle of everyone breathing together, and the ability of an ensemble to find a quiet and centered place from which to begin, is perhaps the most valuable lesson contained in chant and plainsong singing. Our ears become the guide on the journey forward. Sensitivities become keenly heightened, and a renewed sense (almost every rehearsal) of what it means to sing with others is reinforced in every rehearsal.

Summary of Chant Teaching Principles

Below are listed the chant teaching "principles" that are discussed in this chapter. Then what follows is a detailed pedagogical description of each of these teaching principles.

1. Always introduce chants first without text (aural/oral).
2. If the ensemble experiences difficulty with portions of chant, isolate those parts into small "patterns."
3. Break the trance of music notation.
4. Do not group chant into metric "twos" and "threes." This destroys the music intent of chant.
5. Do not add weight to descending notes/gestures.

6. Sing legato through all vocal registers: sing "liquid gold."
7. Always ascend to high notes of the phrase.
8. Remember that motion in chant always continues forward to arrival at ends of phrases.
9. Learn to end phrases: "tucking in."
10. Breath always ends a phrase and begins the next.
11. Eliminate the bar line as a sign of division.
12. Animate the breath; soul-feel the breath.
13. Suspend sound as it moves forward (the performance of repeated tones).
14. Use up/down inflections (impulses).
15. Build intonation listening skills and vocal resonances.
16. Consider the effects of acoustic.
17. Chant moves you to familiar to unfamiliar.
18. Chant teaches resting tone.
19. Know the human meanings of the text.
20. Teach the fantasy of chant.

1. **Always introduce chants first without text (aural/oral).**

> At the aural/oral level, a student learns to recognize a pattern, for example, by hearing it performed usually more than once. Thus, the aural part of aural/oral is activated without the oral part. When students imitate by singing, chanting, and moving to the pattern they have heard, the oral part of aural/oral comes into play. Imitation occurs when students perform what a teacher has performed and when a teacher and student perform together. A student acquires listening vocabularies of tonal patterns and rhythm patterns in the aural part of aural/oral learning and performing vocabularies of tonal patterns and rhythm patterns in the oral part of aural/oral learning. (p. 97)
>
> —Edwin Gordon in
> *Learning Sequences in Music*

As was detailed in an earlier chapter, the principles of Music Learning Theory are all embedded within plainchant. For those singers new to plainchant, the teacher/conductor must always be aware of the processes of music learning that are operating within the students' audiation. For those students unfamiliar with chant and its tonal contexts, *each chant should always be introduced with the teacher chanting and the choir listening.* Included with this book is a solo recorded performance of each chant so the teacher/conductor can learn the chants and their proper musical inflection. This process of music teaching procedure and teaching technique is pivotal to the students' ability to build a powerful audiation "library" of chants—the tonal and phrasing components that can be easily accessed for music making.

> Achievement at the aural/oral level involves continuous back and forth interaction between aural and oral because when students hear tonal patterns and rhythm patterns and sing and chant what they hear, they learn to audiate those patterns and listen to and perform them with understanding. (p. 97)

> —Edwin Gordon
> in *Learning Sequences in Music*

2. If the ensemble experiences difficulty with portions of chant, isolate those parts into small "patterns."

We have learned that a musician's vocabulary is acquired in a similar way to language acquisition—that is, one's ability to hear patterns in a musical context is acquired through smaller fragments of music that are analogous to words in language. If the ensemble is experiencing problems in singing back portions of a chant, immediately isolate shorter "cells" (or patterns) embedded within the chant that seem to be causing difficulty and repeat those several times, with the teacher/conductor singing first and the choir imitating in turn. When the ensemble performs them with good intonation, then return to the plainchant being sung. Whenever there are aural difficulties with any portion of a plainchant, immediately isolate, model, and have the choir sing that fragment in repetition. This is an important step in the music learning process; it should never be omitted if the choir's performance seems to demand some additional focused work on specific patterns embedded within the plainchant.

3. Break the trance of music notation.

> Our main object is to give the phrase life and yet to keep it on as smooth a curve as possible. We must both ascend and descend in the most even and musical way we can. The music must remain in constant motion. (p. 537)

> —Marc Mostovoy
> in Laila Storch, *Marcel Tabuteau*

In a musician's attempts to notate music as accurately as possible the past seven hundred years, we have perhaps inadvertently worked against providing singers and players with a notational system that does not shackle music expressiveness. Bar lines, meter signatures, phrasing markings, articulation markings, dynamic and "breath" marks have created a system that relys on eye rather than ear. Perhaps the most restrictive visual that has been created in our notational system is the bar line. For some reason, as performance with "modern" notation has evolved, performers have added additional weight to whatever is sounded immediately after the bar line. Weight that has nothing to do with text stress or shape of line stops, or rather halts, the forward movement of sound and narrows the trajectory of both the musical line and its inherent expressivity toward a melodic idea.

Additionally, the varying colors of note heads (from hollow to dark) and the beaming of quicker moving music values has moved our art away from an aural art to a visual one. This, perhaps, would not be all that bad if the notational system had more to do with the sound of the music than with its mathematical relationships. In our attempt to notate with accuracy, we have created a notational system that has straightjacketed musicianship and promoted an emphasis upon seeing rather than listening and hearing. Certainly this system has lessened the importance of community and ensemble, and inadvertently seems to place responsibility on individuals.

The approach advocated in this book returns musicians to reading original notation, or at the very least a semi-modern adaptation of that notation without the shackles of bar lines and other notational biases. Gregorian, and to some degree plainchant, notation relies on an approximate notational system that allows for a fluidity of rhythm that is limited only by the skill and imagination of the performers. Distances in the notation imply approximate rhythmic values. The musical designs are mostly diatonic without cadential pulls as we now know them, just cadential formulae. In modern days, we must understand much theory to derive meaning from the notation. In chant, we can derive meaning from the sound around us, and the notation serves as a guide, with text serving as musical "sign posts."

4. Do not group chant into metric "twos" and "threes." This destroys the music intent of chant.

There seems to be a commonly held myth among conductors and those who "teach" chant that the first thing that should be done is that the chant should be analyzed and one should group all the notes of the chant into groupings of twos and threes. By doing so, we may make the chant "easier to conduct," but when such divisional organizations are superimposed onto the chant, we superimpose a very unnatural metric organization that interferes with the forward movement of line that comes with using text to guide musical expression. Under no circumstances should these units of twos or threes be imposed upon chant. The imposition of such a subjective meter adds an unnatural weight and stress, and perhaps accent, and this slows the forward movement of musical line. This deeply disturbs the musical and aural aesthetic of the chant. While there are allusions to groupings of twos and threes, these groupings should grow out of natural text stresses rather than maintaining a strict and rigid subdivision of the beat.

5. Do not add weight to descending notes/gestures.

> A drop in the melody should never give the impression of being
> vertical but should be rounded or curved. Gregorian art is like
> Romanesque art and avoids sharp angles. There must be no yielding
> to a kind of attraction from below with a tendency to hasten the
> speed. Each note must be given its full time value; this in itself will
> produce the right effect. (p. 75)

> —Dom Joseph Gajard
> in *The Solesmes Method*

For some reason, we have been taught to give notes at the bottom of a melodic
curve in modern notation not only added weight, but also emphasis. Chant can re-
align our music sensibilities to make the descent to lower notes without added weight
of musical gesture. Lower notes are part of the shaping of the contour of the line,
but they never denote a weighted change of direction. As will be related a bit later in
this chapter with quotes by Marcel Tabuteau, breath provides an upward energy for
musical line. Lower notes should never receive additional weight and should never be
louder (which is the common musical tendency of most singers due, in part, to added
weight). If anything, lower notes in a melodic contour should be sung with a bit less
weight so the line can spin upward out of that lower melodic curve.

6. Sing legato through all vocal registers: sing "liquid gold."

One of the most important lessons in studying and singing chant is the
realization of how true legato singing is intimately bound to the forward movement
of line without weight. Gabriel Crouch, a former member of the King's Singers, has
implored my singers in the past to sing with "liquid gold." For some reason, the use
of the term "liquid gold" allows the choir to discover for themselves a legato that
is beautiful and that is resonantly balanced enough to carry sound forward. Also,
because focus is on making the line fluid and forward moving, vocal registers seem
to magically mix into a "liquid gold" resonance. Part of this miracle is bound to the
fact that the choir is continually reminded *not* to add any weight to lower notes.

7. Always ascend to high notes of the phrase.

> And so I beg of you, singers, to allow the accent to keep its native lightness at all costs. Do not hammer it out, do not make of it something material or heavy; launch it and give it its full scope. To achieve this, any heavy or incisive stress must be avoided. Lighten the accent, soften it, round it off, broaden it a little. Let it hover, so to speak before the melody alights on the last syllable of the word. It must be discreet, supple, soft, immaterial, "a luminous point which readily appears on the crest of phrases." (p. 47)
>
> —Dom Joseph Gajard
> in *The Solesmes Method*

Ascent rather than *accent* is a difficult habit to break in singers who have derived musical meaning and indirect phrasing ideas from modern notation. High notes do not necessarily equal the climax of phrase; in fact, they almost never do this in chant. "High notes" or "high points" of the phrase should outline the arch and trajectory of the phrase, and high points should be taught and reinforced as notes to be "sung through" rather than "sung on" with weight or accent. The tops of phrases should be sung "through," and sound should always move forward. A distinction should be made between arrival and emphasis. The former implies a cadence, where the latter implies a musical lengthening of the note but does not interrupt the line.

8. Remember that motion in chant always continues forward to arrival at ends of phrases.

> Saint Augustine called rhythm "the art of beautiful movement," and this art is strikingly illustrated in the chant, for while rhythm is free from the restrictions of mathematical measurement, it is alive with beautifully ordered movement. (p. 10)
>
> —Mary Goodchild
> in *Gregorian Chant for Church and School*

> Rather than a "line," a chant melisma should be thought of as a succession of still moments not coming from anywhere, not going anywhere. The choir should sound as if it could stop at any instant in the melisma and remain at that moment forever. The melisma is a kind of study in the paradox of stillness of motion. The voices move but give the effect of not moving. At any moment in the melody, the "present moment" is the only moment of consequence. (p. 78)
>
> —Rembert Herbert
> in *Entrances*

Modern notation has worked against the development of an intuitive sense of phrasing that grows out of the arch of the line and text rather than a visual depiction on a stave. While consistently honest forward motion may be a simple concept, forward motion without pushing or forcing line forward requires a rather aware sense of "letting go" and "allowing" that, in turn, empowers sung sound to move forward in a natural and organic way. Sound can move forward by uploading weight, which then must be released. In chant, animating the breath at the start of the phrase allows the phrase to acquire a natural upward momentum that is both honest and capable of sustaining a beautiful resonance and legato, without weight pushing sound forward. Forward motion is difficult for many singers because of a learned sense of control. Chant teaches us to "allow" sound to move forward within the company of others. It teaches us that sound is truly a manifestation of how we function as musicians within the company of others. Learning to let go and allowing sound to move forward through breath energy is one of the great lessons that chant teaches us as long as we allow ourselves to be taught by sound. Thought of another way, the nature of the notation of chant forces us to sing with direction of line.

9. Learn to end phrases: "tucking in."

At times, the selection of certain words awakes a rather sophisticated concept in singers that is remarkable in its simplicity. In teaching chant to singers, teaching how to complete a musical idea at the end of a phrase poses the biggest challenge.

We have stumbled onto the verbiage of "tucking in" the end of a phrase to arrive at a natural relation and de-emphasis of a phrase. The effect of "tucking in" the end of a phrase happens naturally when singers mentally prepare for the next line of text. Think of it like inflection in speech (or musical inflections in psalmody). This then refers singers back to the text and unstressed syllables that need "tucking in." "Tucking in" becomes synonymous with unstressed syllables at the ends of phrases.

10. Breath always ends a phrase and begins the next.

One of the most important phrasing concepts ensembles must learn is to listen for each other's breath and to learn to breathe together. Active inhalation must begin immediately as the previous phrase is "tucked in." Finishing phrases of chant will take care of themselves. Phrase endings are created by the immediate and instinctual start of an animated and energized breath that begins the next melodic shape or phrase. This concept of connecting phrases with breath—sound connects into breath and begins sound—is central not only to the performance of chant, but with any music performance that has degree of honesty born out of a sense of ensemble.

11. Eliminate the bar line as a symbol of division.

One of the doorways to artistic phrasing is to acknowledge that anything following a bar line does not receive weighted accent or stress. The printing of bar lines provides a subliminal visual barrier to the forward movement of sound. This principle of avoiding adding weight after the bar line was central to the phrasing system developed by Marcel Tabuteau at the Curtis Institute. Chant re-teaches us through notation that sound moves constantly forward. Since there are no bar lines in chant, we do not risk bringing bar line associations from modern music making into our music making.

12. Animate the breath; soul-feel the breath.[11]

Inhale/Exhale

It is always two elements that create a meaning. Your line (phrase) is a continuous disturbance of inhale and exhale. Music is living and must breathe. Everything occurs in pairs: High tide/Low tide; day/night; inhaling/exhaling, etc.; that is life. (p. 541)

—Marcel Tabuteau
in Laila Storch,
Marcel Tabuteau

13. Suspend sound as it moves forward (the performance of repeated tones).

By the way they are sung, sustained notes often immobilize the melody and give an impression of halts and interruptions in the rhythmic flow. But they too must take part in the life of the group or phrase by tending towards what follows in an appropriate crescendo or decrescendo. In other words, there must be no immobilized notes or halts but held notes that are "on the move." (p. 80)

—Dom Joseph Gajard
in *The Solesmes Method*

One of the most important ideas that chant can teach us has to do with the performance of repeated notes. For some reason, repeated notes seem to accrue individual weighted accents as we sing them. Each repeated note becomes an event rather than a connected event that moves sound consistently forward without the addition of weight. Momentum moves sound forward; velocity moves sound forward; *weight and emphasis do not*. Also, understanding the role of repeated notes in the context of a broader musical shape is what chant teaches us. The momentum of moving sound forward as one sings with a group can be revelatory if we allow it to be. We can only accomplish this by truly listening to others.

---

11   These phrases are borrowed from a lecture by Nova Thomas that can be seen on the DVD, *The Musician's Breath* (GIA).

14. Use up/down inflections (impulses).

> You can have up inflections and down inflections. Inhales are up in feeling, exhales are down in feeling. Up equals energy—down equals weight. Downs are heavier than ups. Before you have a down inflection, you should go up. An inflection up is suspense, when you go up you must come down unless (you wish to remain) suspended. (p. 541)

> —Marcel Tabuteau
> in Laila Storch,
> *Marcel Tabuteau*

Chant teaches us to emphasize upward motion of sound to propel and move sound forward. Conducting chant (chironomy) places a gestural importance upon both horizontal gesture and upward gesture. When chanting, it is often helpful for the singers to conduct themselves using upward gestures that are largely devoid of weight.

15. Build intonation listening skills and vocal resonance.

> The special quality of intonation is produced by resonance: in dwelling on the same pitch the sound can re-sound; the pulses of the sound traveling through the air can restrike the ear at a constant rate (frequency), reinforcing its effect in a marvelous way. Resonance is basic in many modes of human experience. A simple but vivid example is pushing a child in a swing: when the push exactly matches the momentum of the swing, the motion of the swing builds up much faster and greater than it would otherwise. Even more vivid is resonance in sound, once you become sensitive to it: resonance is responsible for music's most common characteristics—as well as its most magical effects. (p. 26)

> —Richard L. Crocker
> in *An Introduction to Gregorian Chant*

One of the more fascinating observations I made as my ensemble grappled with chant both at Oxford and at home in Westminster was the idea of resonance. For some reason, at first everyone's initial "vocal assumption" was to perform the chants in a stylized and restricted resonance style. That is, lighter, almost off-the-breath singing seemed to be the default. The choir seemed to want to maintain this somewhat "white" sound throughout the chants. What I noticed was that both musical line and intonation suffered. It has been my experience (limited as it is with chant) that that was the way chant was to be done. I mistakenly assumed that reining in the tone, even limiting it to a more forward format, was the way to go. No one told me that, I just went there with no thought process because of unfounded biases in my audiation of what chant should "sound like."

My instincts told me something was the matter from not only a vocal standpoint, but also a spiritual one. One of my singers stayed after rehearsal and related his experiences to singing chant at St. Clement's Church in Philadelphia. The choir at St. Clement's is one of the finer choirs I know. Peter Conte directs the singers there. My singer who sings in that choir said, "We sing with a fully resonant sound." In talking with Peter, he relayed that he allows the singers "on-the-breath" singing at all times when chanting.[12] The contemplative aspect of the text, and the singer serving as delivering the text, is what gives chant its simple nature and sound. It should not be soloistic like opera. However, it should always be sung with great energy and healthy singing, not off the voice.

So with those mental adjustments in mind a few weeks into the process, we changed how we sang and allowed the sound to find its own "resonantial" way. It has always been my belief that limiting resonance directly affects the ability of a singer or an ensemble to move a musical line, or musical sound, forward. By "opening up" the resonance and sound of the ensemble, the effects of resonance, especially on repeated pitches, create sheer magic in both sound and line.

16. Consider the effects of acoustic.

There was another incredible discovery I took away from our chanting during all phases of the Choral Institute at Oxford. Our "classroom space" was the church that is part of St. Stephen's House, a hall of the University at Oxford. It is a stunningly beautiful space and architecturally quite expansive.

---

12   For those reading at this point who do not understand the term "singing on the breath," it implies that breath is fully engaged throughout the singing process, thus allowing for a lower laryngeal position, which allows for a fuller resonance possibility in the voice. For specific techniques to develop on-the-breath singing, the reader is referred to *The Choral Warm-Up* (GIA).

As I listened to the choir and conductors grapple with singing chant, I noticed that intonation became a function of overtones sounded by the room and that, in fact, the choir's intonational sense was developed because of the room's ability to retain overtones and sustain implied harmonic structures contained in the chant (e.g., tonic, subdominant). For me, it was clear that by pressing the choir to *listen,* chant allowed the room to instruct them in what is "good" intonation. The quote that follows is a bit more succinct.

> A reverberant acoustic space can reinforce certain components of a sound selectively, making these components much more noticeable. Under most conditions any intoned pitch produces overtones, certain other pitches that are higher but that blend in well with the fundamental [tone]—so well that they are usually not noticed. The first and second overtones are strong in the human voice, and are sometimes audible under ordinary circumstances; in a reverberant space they can be greatly magnified, increasing the power of the sound. A cathedral or other reverberant space may magnify the overtones selectively, producing remarkable effects. Our idea of Gregorian Chant should include the possibilities of these dimensions of sound. (p. 27)
>
> —Richard L. Crocker
> in *An Introduction to Gregorian Chant*

The Westminster Williamson Voices ensemble rehearses in Bristol Chapel at Westminster Choir College. The acoustics of that room lend themselves to the acoustic principles discussed above. To create more of an acoustic "ambiance," we place women on one side of the chapel and men on the other side. Without doubt, a reverberant or "wet" room is part of the alchemy of building musicianship of the ensemble through listening to each other.

17. Chant moves you to familiar to unfamiliar.

Part of the issue of building musical listening skill is based upon a tenet of Music Learning Theory, but I believe, in this case, the tenet works in reverse. Western ears are culturated to hear predictable patterns of notes in tonic, subdominant, and dominant chord structures that are embedded in major tonality for the vast majority of inexperienced singers, and singers in general. In American culture, major tonality is our default for pitch recognition and for *tuning*. Chant shuffles our aural deck a bit because pitches in Gregorian melodies and plainchant melodies are unfamiliar to the ear because they imply modes. Moreover, because of the repetition of chant "patterns," new modes and patterns remain in our ears and also sound in the room. In essence, chant builds audiation[13] skill with respect to modes and modal tuning. Thus, chant expands the aural vocabulary of any ensemble by teaching the ensemble what something is by what it is not...major! This inferential type of music learning is a necessity for the development of music skill. Again, another way of analyzing this audiation phenomenon:

> The imprint of pitches in memory is a complex and extremely important phenomenon: it forms the context in which we understand the melody. This context seems always to be present and operative when we listen to music. The ear can hear more than the pitch that is actually sounding; it can hear, in memory, the preceding pitches as well. This makes it possible to hear in Gregorian chant a network of pitch relationships, not just single pitches. (p. 30)
>
> —Richard L. Crocker
> in *An Introduction to Gregorian Chant*

18. Chant teaches resting tone.

Perhaps no skill is as vital to the development of a musician as the skill of knowing the resting tone of the mode that one is singing "on" or "in." "On" a mode is the modality that one is currently singing within, acknowledging that a chant changes its mode. Such chants are indeed rare, but they do exist. Hildegard von Bingen developed a complex system of modal "modulation" that was used by her as an expressive and tone painting device. The ability to know, or rather audiate,

---

13   *Audiation* is a term coined by Edwin Gordon over 40 years ago to describe the multi-dimensional perceptual act of hearing a sound without it actually being present. Gordon defines audiation as "hearing and comprehending in one's mind sound of music not, or may never have been, physically present (p. 389), *Learning Sequences in Music.*

resting tone is fundamental to the development of intonation. Without the ability to audiate a resting tone *and* retain the resting tone of the mode one is in is the only way to develop not only individual intonation, but a stable sense of ensemble intonation. Because of the repetitive and musical "cell" construction of chant, it develops a strong sense of resting tone because the chants tend to return to the "reference" tone and create a strong modal stability in one's audiation because of the frequent reinforcement of the resting tone. In essence, chant contains its own built-in "oral/aural" level of learning.[14]

19. Know the human meanings of the text.

While the purpose of chant was to express the meaning of the text, singers must be reminded to search for not only literal meanings of the texts they sing, but also universal meanings of what is being sung. The musical (and communal) nuances of chant stem from the treatment of the text and innermost clarity of human expression. To reach this "honest place" of musical expression, we must be able to take an inner journey of meaning that is best accomplished through communities of musicians engaging in a monophonic expression of a unison idea. Intonation will always suffer if there is not some degree of "agreement" on what is being expressed. In *The Musician's Breath* (GIA), my co-author Nova Thomas developed a language to remind singers to sing with honest expression and maintain an awareness of how that expression is connected to breath. Meaning is uploaded into musical expression through an *inspiration that is inspired*. She reminds us to *fix the idea and not necessarily the sound*. And finally, as we sing chant, we need to constantly remind ourselves that *breath is the body's theater*.

---

14 Within the Music Learning Theory detailed by Edwin Gordon, aural/oral is the most important level of music learning. It is where sounds are heard, audiated, and retained in audiation without the use of notation. The most potent and long-term music learning takes place within the aural/oral level of music learning.

20. Teach the fantasy of chant.

I think we would all agree that musical imagination is an important "skill" for any musician. Because the musical materials are so limited in chant, I have found that it is easier to ignite group musical imagination. There is something deeply centered and enriching about a group of singers making a journey together with chant as their forward-moving "device." Chant allows singers to shape as they see fit the curves, the rises, and the falls of the chant, and to use its forward motion as expression. The tendency for any group is to "slow down." In chant, slowing occurs when one or more singers are not listening or, rather, are not aware of what is going on around them. *Chant does not allow singers to disconnect from either the sound at the moment, the sound that has passed, or themselves!* Chant teaches those skills better than any other instructional delivery system I know. The sound world of chant embedded within an acoustic allows the development of a sense of musical fantasy about sound—a quality of sound that is both direct and honest because it is born out of a community of people.

CHAPTER 10
USING EFFORT/SHAPE TO EXPERIENCE PLAINCHANT

Marcel Tabuteau said: "I have always been in favor to play as I think. Of course, the ideal combination would be to play with *thinking* and *intelligent feeling*."

—Marcel Tabuteau in David McGill,
Sound in Motion

A true musician believes only in what he hears. No matter how ingenious theory is, it means nothing to him until the evidence is placed before him in actual sound. (p. 156)

—Paul Hindemith in
The Craft of Musical Composition, Vol. 1

W e know that for musicians, our bodily kinesthesia, or the feeling of movement, is both taught and reinforced by our aural conception of how music moves forward. And we know that through neuroscience those feelings bonded to musical sounds are stored for retrieval for our day-to-day music making. Through my experience I have found that previously learned kinesthesia associated with the forward movement of musical line and the shaping of that musical line can interfere or severely bias the creation of new musical ideas and musical expressions. While our musical self might want to sing or play a certain musical idea informed by the music or the text, previous kinesthetic "learning" and "memory" bonded to similar phrasing ideas will influence not only phrasing, but also pitch and rhythm in a negative, almost delimiting way.

Because chant exposes us to a "new" phrasing experience, our mirror neurons must be reprogrammed so that what we hear is bonded to a new kinesthesia in our bodies...a type of "movement learning." Sound and the "feeling" within us are incredibly powerful resources within musicians. Sound is movement and movement is sound—and *both* are bonded together in audiation. Any pedagogy that does not teach to both modalities will either slow or deeply confound musical learning.

The Laban Efforts and Their Intimate Relationship to Chant

Regarding movement learning for musicians, as music is sounded by us, an immediate kinesthetic "map" is put on file within our bodies *if* we are aware that such imprinting is taking place with the performance of every phrase. If we do not realize that such an associative imprinting is taking place, then previous kinesthesia learned from other music is mistakenly associated with and superimposed upon the new music being sung. How music moves forward and its feeling within the body is always felt while music is being performed. Considering that, while this new world of plainchant and singing with others is being taught, it is important to acknowledge an awareness of how we feel as we are performing chant and allow it to assume an important part in our plainchant experience. As with anything else, it is important to be able to label kinesthetic feelings, and Laban Effort/Shape terminology provides that invaluable pedagogical labeling tool.

Identifying the Effort/Shape Qualities of Chant

The Laban Effort Elements: Flow, Weight, Time, and Space

Movement is more than a change of location of the body or a change in the position of the body limbs. There are changes in speed, changes in direction, changes in focus, and changes in the energy associated with different movements. Consequently, there is a constant fluctuation in levels of exertion. Laban defined exertion in movement as the interrelationship of flow, weight, time, and space, which he called the Effort Elements. For each of the four Effort Elements, Laban identified a pair of extremes, which he called "qualities," with the idea that the quality of each element of a given movement could be described in relation to its placement on a continuum that extends between those two extremes.

Flow is the variation in the quality of bodily tension that underlies all of the Effort Elements. The extremes of flow are free and bound. Free flow allows body energy to move through and out beyond the body boundaries without any restriction. Ideal free flow movement is difficult to stop. A person experiencing total free flow would be difficult to stop, weightless and unhampered by tension. Bound flow movement is restrained and can be stopped easily; it forces the mover to contain energy within the body boundary. A person experiencing extreme bound flow would be tense to the point of motionlessness. Between the two extremes of free flow and bound flow are infinite gradations of tension.

Weight is the sensation of force or burden exerted in a movement. The extremes of weight are light and heavy. Light movement can be described as delicate and overcomes the sensation of body weight. Heavy movement is forceful and uses the sensation of body weight to make an impact. A person must sense the quality of his or her movements as being either light or heavy. Central to one's understanding, and consequently to one's understanding of rhythm, is the ability to sense involuntary changes in one's own body weight as well as the ability to change weight at will.

Time relates to the expenditure or duration of time in a movement. The extremes of time are sustained and quick. Sustained time is prolonging, lingering, or decelerating. Quick time contains a sense of urgency and rapidity. For musicians, the Effort Element of time is closely related to tempo.

Space is the manner in which energy is focused in a movement. The extremes of space are either direct or indirect. Indirect movement involves a flexible but all-encompassing attention to the environment. Direct movement involves a channeled, singularly focused awareness of the environment. The element of space is closely related to the concept of focus. Is the space in which a movement takes place focused or spread? Do all body parts focus to a central point, or are they dispersed?

One might think of the Effort Elements of flow, weight, time, and space as the how, what, when, and where of movement.

Experiencing the Efforts in Combination

It is easiest to gain an understanding of the Effort Elements through their various combinations as suggested by Laban. It is difficult to experience flow, weight, time, or space separately. By adjusting the relative intensities of flow, weight, time, and space within an activity, one can relate an infinite variety of movement possibilities. Laban assigned an action verb to each combination of three of the Effort Elements. Central to his theory is the simultaneous concentration on the three elements of weight, space, and time taking over, or predominating, changes in flow. Laban's action verbs, which describe combinations of the Effort Elements, along with movement examples for each verb are shown on the next page. The abbreviations denote S = Space, W = Weight, and T = Time.

For each of the Efforts in Combination, the elements of time, space, and weight interact to produce the illusion of flow. That is, the perception of one's rhythmic and gestural flow is a by-product of the interaction of time, space, and weight. Flow cannot exist alone. It is the result of infinite combinations of time, weight, and space, which produces an infinite variety of movement. The genius of Laban is the ability to observe how the combinations of time, space, and weight can be varied to produce what is perceived as flow. These principles are important to conductors to make them aware of the infinite potential of their own movement and to reawaken movement within themselves that may not have been used since childhood, or to reawaken movement that may not be part of their current life experience.

Laban Efforts in Combination to Describe Movement

Laban Action Verb (Elements)	Qualities	Movement Examples
float	indirect (S) light (W) sustained (T)	treading water at various depths
wring	indirect (S) heavy (W) sustained (T)	wringing a beach towel
glide	direct (S) light (W) sustained (T)	smoothing wrinkles in a cloth ice skating
press	direct (S) heavy (W) sustained (T)	pushing a car
flick	indirect (S) light (W) quick (T)	dusting off lint from clothing
slash	indirect (S) heavy (W) quick (T)	fencing serving a tennis ball
dab	direct (S) light (W) quick (T)	typing tapping on a window
punch	direct (S) heavy (W) quick (T)	boxing

Laban believed that to become adept with movement, one should develop a daily routine of exploring the Efforts in Combination. In the initial stages of movement exploration, the "labeling" and understanding of the Effort Element content in everyday life activities provide the foundation of movement understanding because it grows out of one's personal experience. Laban believed that we have all experienced a complete spectrum of movement possibilities as children, but we have forgotten those movement experiences because the routine of our daily lives has minimized our daily movement experience. For each of the Combinations shown on the previous page, there are suggestions of life activities that would reawaken that particular Effort Combination within the conductor. Mime each of the suggestions for each category and discover how a change in one or more of the individual Effort Elements changes the movement. Add your personal experiences to each list.

Experiences of Efforts in Combination

Float
indirect (space)
light (weight)
sustained (time)

- tracing a picture with a pencil
- floating in a pool on your back
- vaulting over a high bar by means of a pole
- using a bubble wand
- spraying a room with air freshener
- lying on a waterbed
- falling into the first moments of sleep
- reaching for an unfamiliar cat
- staggering
- swinging on a rope swing
- blowing bubbles
- Other:

Wring
indirect (space)
heavy (weight)
sustained (time)

- twisting a washcloth dry
- twisting a sweater dry
- twisting hair in the morning
- twisting a face cloth
- drying out a sponge
- twisting off a bottle cap
- opening a cardboard can of prepackaged cookie dough
- washing socks
- playing with a hula hoop
- drying your hands under a blower
- tightening a jar cap
- turning over dirt with a trowel
- squeezing juice from an orange
- twisting a twist tie on a garbage bag
- using a screwdriver
- pulling out the stem of an apple
- spinning a dreidel
- opening a can of sardines
- using a melon baller
- opening a stuck faucet handle
- massaging a muscle
- Other:

Press
direct (space)
heavy (weight)
sustained (time)

- kissing a child gently
- pushing a shopping cart loaded with groceries
- ironing a shirt
- pressing a button on a drink machine
- pushing a child on a swing
- squeezing a tennis ball

- pressing on the floor when doing a handstand
- closing an overloaded suitcase
- pushing a lawnmower in high grass
- pushing a lawnmower up hill
- using a paper cutter
- using a hole punch
- pushing in a laundromat coin cartridge
- moving a piano
- pedaling a mountain bike up hill
- applying the brakes on a car
- kneading dough for bread
- removing a childproof cap
- walking with an umbrella against the wind
- washing a window with a squeegee
- stapling papers
- using a clothespin
- ringing a doorbell
- pushing in a thumbtack
- using a screwdriver
- packing trash in a filled garbage bag
- using a mechanical hand drill
- going through a revolving door
- closing a car trunk lid when the trunk is very full
- making mashed potatoes
- buckling a seat belt
- Other:

Glide
direct (space)
light (weight)
sustained (time)

- reaching to shake hands
- wiping up a spill with a paper towel
- pushing off from the side of a pool and moving forward
- ice skating
- erasing a blackboard
- dusting or wiping off a table
- drawing a violin bow across one string

- spreading butter or jelly on toast
- gently scratching your arm
- sliding down a banister
- coasting down a hill on a bicycle
- roller-blading or roller-skating
- throwing a paper airplane
- sliding in socks on a newly polished floor
- painting a wall with a roller
- opening a sliding glass door
- smoothing the sheets when making a bed
- dusting furniture with a feather duster
- putting a ring on your finger
- closing a zip-lock sandwich bag
- turning a page in a book
- smoothing cement with a trowel
- water skiing or snow skiing
- icing a cake
- drawing a circle with a compass
- playing a glissando on a piano
- sliding on an icy sidewalk
- shaving
- Other:

Dab
direct (space)
light (weight)
quick (time)

- putting the final touches on the frosting of a cake
- tip-toeing
- playing darts (moment the dart is released from the hand)
- using a paint brush to make dots
- poking someone's arm with a finger
- dipping a cloth in a pail of water
- breaking a balloon with a pin
- knocking ash off a cigarette
- dotting an "i"
- applying antiseptic on a small cut

- tap-dancing
- pushing a button on a remote control
- typing
- finger-painting
- using touch-up paint
- testing hot water with your finger
- cleaning cobwebs from the ceiling
- powdering on make-up
- using white glue
- cleaning a child's sticky mouth
- placing a cherry on a sundae
- Other:

Flick
indirect (space)
light (weight)
quick (time)

- removing an insect off the table
- turning a light switch on or off
- leafing through the pages of a book
- lightly keeping a balloon in the air
- brushing debris off a desk or table
- shooing a fly
- wiping sweat from the brow
- shooting marbles
- touching a hot stove
- throwing a frisbee
- snapping your fingers
- opening "flip-top" toothpaste
- brushing snow from a windshield
- lighting a cigarette lighter
- taking a basketball foul shot
- striking a match
- folding egg whites
- throwing rice
- popping soap bubbles
- Other:

Slash
indirect (space)
heavy (weight)
quick (time)

- swinging a baseball bat
- fencing
- casting a fishing line
- golfing
- opening a cardboard carton with a utility knife
- wielding a knife like a butcher
- tearing a piece of paper
- using an axe to chop wood
- slamming a door
- shaking catsup from a new bottle
- employing self-defense maneuvers
- sweeping a sandy floor with a push broom
- beating a hanging rug clean
- cutting vegetables
- Other:

Punch
direct (space)
heavy (weight)
quick (time)

- plumping a pillow
- boxing
- using a punching bag
- applauding loudly
- hammering a nail
- pounding a fist on a table
- striking a stapler to get the staple in a hard wall
- digging a hole
- Other:

CHANT POSES UNIQUE PEDGAGOGICAL CHALLENGES
TO TEACHERS AND SINGERS: LEARN HOW TO WITHHOLD WEIGHT

Music performance is intimately bound to kinesthetic feeling within one's body. As William James theorized at the end of the nineteenth century, all rhythm learning is processed thorugh feeling receptors in one's joints. From recent mirror neuron research, we know that sound bonds immediately to a kinesthetic sense that is either acquired through movement or acquired through how it feels to move sound forward.

A major issue in ensembles and with individual musicians is that previously acquired kinesthetic sensations are associated, regardless of harmonic context or text, to music that may be similar to music perfomed in the past. Chant is particularly vulnerable because most singers bring other phrasing experiences and kinesthesa to what they are singing, triggered by notational visual triggers.

In looking at the Laban Efforts in Combination, four of them have a direct relationship with chant, the others less so.

Efforts in Combination Utilized in Chant

Float

Glide

Dab

Press

Efforts in Combination Tangential to Chant

Wring

Punch

Slash

Flick

One of the kinesthetic miracles in ballet training is that the movement training accomplishes a movement that disperses the feeling of weight somewhat evenly. In other words, from a Laban point of view, ballet dancers are taught to withhold weight. In a simimar way, the pedagogical challenge when teaching chant is to move singers into another kinesthetic world where they learn the feeling of *witholding* weight so the musical line spins forward without the encumberance of a musician's tradiational sense of stress. The feeling of witholding weight teaches singing that has a kinesthetic of lightness while spinning sound forward.

Understanding the Movement Physics of the Oval

If we move our hand in a circle, we actually create a kind of parabola, or oval. If we are kinesthetically aware as our hand falls to the bottom of that oval, we feel that the hand increases both weight and speed as it falls toward gravity. If there is no compensation, that pull downward creates a weighted feeling in the hand. That heavy weight is the natural default for downward movement. What must be understood is that we do have the abilty to withhold weight as our hand moves downward, to lighten the pull of gravity, to lessen the weight load of the hand as it naturally accerelerates. This feeling of witholding weight is essential to a kinesthetic understand of how chant moves forward.[15] The ability to both imagine and actually be able to withold weight is fundamental to understanding the performance of chant. It should also be noted that this witholding of weight, or rather the ability to not withold weight, is tied to matters of control deep within us. To sing chant, and to be musical in general, we must be able to allow ourselves the gift of letting go—to allow sound to lead us rather than us pushing sound forward. Make no mistake about it. The ability to allow for the beautiful forward movement of chant line involves us understanding how *not* to control. In musicians, control must be equated with

---

15   Previous in this text is an explanation of the use of Laban for acquiring a broader movement vocabulary regarding the withholding of weight via the Efforts in Combination of Float, Glide, Dab, and Press. For further information and demonstration, the reader is referred to the book and DVD, *The Conductor's Gesture* (GIA).

weight. The ability to "lighten" ourselves in a kinesthetic sense, yet still stay on the breath, is perhaps a new feeling. But that feeling will open up a world of expression that is unimaginable.

USE OF PHYSICAL GESTURE TO COUNTERACT THE INCLINATION TO ADD WEIGHT

It is quite common that musicians weaned on modern notation instinctively add weight after bar lines and when a musical line descends. The "sound" of the weight can be heard as a slowing of forward motion of the line, a "thickening" of the sonic content or color of the sound, or an alteration of pitch. Usually, all three make their appearance. I have found that while singers understand the concept of withholding weight and can hear the effect of the equalization of weight, the visual habits developed from a notational system are enormous. It also must be noted that most of these performance problems relating to a singer's inability to sing a forward-moving line that has an "achitectural shape"—the trajectory of sound to rise and fall—is linked intimately to the learning process. If singers tried to learn their musical skills while they acquired the sounds of music, then notation problems and the artistic performance of musical line becomes deeply confused. Sound and rhythm become married to visual notation in an expressively toxic way. That binding of sound to notation is a difficult bond to break. That is the bad news.

The good news is that it can be broken through several avenues: (1) looking at neume notation while singing; (2) using physical movement to counteract the natural learned tendency to add weight to downward moving melodic lines; and (3) the power of "making yourself less so others can become more" demands that we "join" the forward movement of the line. In a group setting, we will immediately *hear* and *be aware* of those around us who are adding weight to the musical line.

The Power of Horizontal Hand Movement or Circular Ovals to Counteract Weight in Singing Plainchant and Musical Line in General

Using the Laban principles above, physical gesture becomes our best pedagogical allie to re-chart the true and beautiful trajectory of musical line using plainchant. Moving the hand from left to right in a smooth, continuous glide is a powerful antidote to added weight in musical line—in this case, plainchant line. Vertical gestures performed as ovals also have a similar pedagogical aiding effect as long as weight is withheld or avoided at the bottom of the oval gesture.

Both of these movements provide several other pedagogical benefits. Adding physical gesture to sound supports the forward movement of breath, which nourishes and feeds the vocalic flow of the line and supports a healthy way of singing. Such "equalized" weight also allows the laryngeal position to stay relaxed, producing beautiful and free vocal production and a resonance that easily connects to one's spiritual interior. This practice of the use of physical gesture is a mandatory part of the pedagogy present here. For conductors who realize its benefits, the musical yield will be astounding.

The Physics of Plainchant: Ascent and Descent

I have discovered certain "physics" involved with plainchant singing. By and large, in Western music we become accustomed to phrasing in shorter units and using much more "stress" (or weight) in attempting to be "musical." As is addressed in this text, while weight is the enemy of any musical expression, weight will destroy the natural beauty of chant. That is partly the reason why the Laban Efforts of Float, Glide, Dab, and Flick are so important in teaching—to awaken this category of Efforts that has as its common denominator the witholding of weight.

Perhaps the most important factor is the fact that plainchant phrases become "airborne" when two factors interact: When chant is begun with an energized breath, that breath energy propels the musical line of chant on an upward trajectory providing weight is not added, *but rather is withheld,* as the line moves forward. It is the uploading of the proper amount of breath energy at the start of the phrase that determines its trajectory, arch, shape, and descent. Just as one calculates the trajectory of a soccer ball based on the energy of a kick, so, too, does a singer propel or spin sound forward with energy contained in the breath. Once the chant has been "launched," the skill of not adding undue weight or "witholding" weight is a kinesthetic skill that must be well in hand. Efforts that reinforce the kinesthetic of lightness are necessary to begin a movement vocabulary that needs to be accessed for the performance of chant.

CHAPTER 11
WHAT CAN WE LEARN FROM THE EXPERIENCES OF PLAINCHANT?

The way to find the real world is not merely to measure and observe what is outside us, but to discover our own inner ground. For that is where the world is, first of all: in my deepest self. It is a living and self-creating mystery of which I am myself a part, to which I am myself my own unique door. (p. 97)

—Thomas Merton
in *Thinking Through Thomas Merton*

The page can show us a rudimentary graph of rhythm: pulse, accents at measure lines, duple or triple meter, relative tempo. But the interesting ramifications of time cannot be notated. We hear them and respond to them intuitively if not intellectually. Yet they are rarely discussed and so there seems to be no accepted vocabulary to deal with them. (p. 17)

Impossible to notate are the energy fields of the song: how it accumulates and relaxes as the song moves through time and tone. (p. 18)

—Alice Parker
in *The Answering Voice*

Because the eye gazes but can catch no glimpse of it,

It is called elusive.

Because the ear listens but cannot hear it,

It is called rarified.

Because the hand feels for it but cannot find it,

It is called infinitesimal…

These are called the shapeless shapes,

Forms without form,

Vague semblances.

Go towards them, and you can see no front;

Go after them and you can see no rear. (p. 71)

—Lao-tzu
in C. G. Jung, *Synchronicity*

A few people there are who regard attempted analysis as attempted murder. It is true that with words one can describe the shape of a tune, but not convey a sense of its practical emotional effect; that texture can be analyzed to some extent, but its quality be known only through living sounds. Yet there is a taint of humbug in the wholesale condemnation of attempts to examine the means by which a composer attains his ends. In the end, all works are subjected to analysis; and not without real profit. But knowledge so gained is, or ought to be, only complementary. (p. v)

—Herbert Howells in Cooke and Maw,
The Music of Herbert Howells

Perhaps the quote immediately above from Herbert Howells best details the musical challenge to conductors. Analysis and description have become the conductor's primary tools rather than experience and musical intuition that is a product of those experiences. It is perhaps inappropriate to begin with a summary, but in short, notation should only be a *complementary* tool or aid at best. One's ear and kinesthetic sensibility should at all times be the *only* (or at least the primary) informant of gestural decisions. Notation can only lead a conductor on a path that disguises and morphs the intuitive and natural tendencies within a phrase. Plainchant gives us both the aural and kinesthetic experience and confidence through musical idea to rely on what is heard and felt rather than what is seen. Further, if we allow these newfound melodic shapes to ride on and be informed by harmonic rhythm,[16] then a dynamic of music making is uncovered that reveals, in every case, the deepest soulful intent of the composer.

INTRODUCTION OR CONCLUSION—OR BOTH?

In most books, one usually turns to the final chapter for conclusions and implications of the book for application to one's work in the future. In many ways, this chapter could serve a good purpose if it appeared at the beginning of this book. But the implications of what chant teaches are so far-reaching that it would take considerable time for digestion and assimilation. The questions most frequently asked of me are, "Why should I study chant?" and "What does chant have to do with what and how I teach my choir?" Moreover, "How does chant influence conducting?"

READJUSTING HOW YOU HEAR AND EXPERIENCE MUSIC

Perhaps the biggest change I experienced was giving myself permission to "vision" music and, consequently, to hear music. I have long been aware of the music learning problems and the severe visual obstacles that written notation poses

---

16 Harmonic rhythm, by definition, is the rate of speed that harmony moves forward. Harmonic rhythm is different from chord progression. While chord progression is a labeling device, harmonic rhythm exists in sound and is a perceivable quality. The term was first used by Walter Piston in his book *Harmony*. The book *Conducting Technique Etudes* (GIA) utilizes exercises that are structured to train conductors to respond to harmonic rhythm first. Harmonic rhythm coupled with an experiential knowledge of the performance of chant is an invaluable tool for conductors.

for the teaching and learning of music. It has been established that any attempt to read notation before there is an aural music vocabulary in place severely limits not only one's musical growth but also one's musicianship.

Until recently, I was unaware to what extent notation affects how we cause music to happen through our conducting and performing the very same music as singers. Modern notation is an obstacle for conductors because it flies in the face of natural and organic music making. Conducting, more or less, is a kinesthetic/physical movement art form that *should* guide and help move sound forward. Through chant I have discovered—or perhaps better stated, re-discovered—the kinesthetic and aural journey that musical line can provide if we allow ourselves to take that journey without the encumbrances of modern notation and harmonic structure. Moreover, I am convinced that elements of musicianship can be best introduced and taught through the communal sounding of a monophonic line through plainchant. The impact of sounding chant within a community is one of the most powerful teaching tools we can have in our self-educational arsenal.

MUSICAL WILL

Creativity is allowing yourself to make mistakes. Art is knowing which ones to keep. (p. 37)

—Scott Adams in Sarah Louis,
The Rise

To know and then not to know is the greatest puzzle of all…So much preparation for a few moments of innocence—of desperate play. To learn how to unlearn. (p. 141)

—Philip Guston in Sarah Louis,
The Rise

Not known, because not looked for

But heard, half heard, in the stillness

Between two waves of the sea.

Quick now, here, now, always—

A condition of complete simplicity

(Costing not less than everything)…

—T. S. Eliot
from *Four Quartets*

It may sound a bit ridiculous, but the old educational adage that you have to "know what something isn't before you know what it is" most succinctly describes my experience with plainchant. I thought I understood musical line, and I *really* thought I understood "conducting." The chant experience has re-informed and re-educated me by showing me what musical line is *not*. Plainchant, in essence, has become my new "safe haven" for true exploration of what it means to be both musically expressive and honest.

Conductors (and singers) use what I call "musical will" to move their own sung or played sound forward, or conductors mistakenly use *improperly weighted* gesture to move—or rather, push—sound forward. The first and perhaps most important lesson of chant is that music making, at its optimum point of expressivity, comes from a humble place where one becomes less so others and the *music* can become more. The Williamson Voices singers, who sing chant to begin every rehearsal, soon find out that if their "being isn't right," the musical "doing" does not come easily. Rhythm problems and intonation problems abound when we are not in the right "spiritual" or "human" place to allow music to come through us. It is a profoundly remarkable experience when a choir performs plainchant. There needs to be a calm in the rehearsal space that creates an intense atmosphere for *listening* and for an *awareness* of sound and others. And perhaps most importantly, the awareness of one's own breath and the breath of others turns one's attention toward the magic that happens in the moment of breath. Musical will transforms itself from being an act of control and will to a deeply moving act of becoming part of something larger than oneself within an envelope of sound. One discovers that sound will move if energized through breath. One learns that sound cannot and should not be controlled, but rather allowed.

Plainchant teaches us a willful way of allowing rather than making, of listening loudly to others and breathing together in a way that binds us together as a community of musicians and artists into a powerful and compelling common expression. I have found the experience of plainchant liberating, deeply calming, and connecting—and most importantly, it has given me a new aural and kinesthetic "map" for how we *really* sing a truly honest and compelling musical phrase. Chant, more so than any other "pedagogy," teaches us how to "allow ourselves to be" so music comes from our deepest selves.

CHANT: AN INNER TEMPLATE FOR BELONGING— EXPRESSION GROWS FROM A DEEPLY INTERIOR PLACE

It is not as an author that I would speak to you, not as a storyteller, not as a philosopher, not as a friend only: I seek to speak to you in some way as your own self. Who can tell what this may mean? I myself do not know. But if you listen, things will be said that are perhaps not written in this book. And this will be due not to me, but to the One who lives and speaks in both of us. (p. 35)

—Thomas Merton
in *Thinking through Thomas Merton*

One of the great lessons that chant provides is that the community of singers is unable to sing until the "community" is right—in a human way. In many ways, we have to acknowledge that there needs to be a kind of "inner template" for our way of being with each other. We must learn that our way of being together has everything to do with the music we make. Chant teaches us this, almost immediately, because its very sound is a musical expression born out of and from a community of people. That community of people truly teaches us a human awareness of others through sound. When the energy is not right among and between the people in the room, that instability rears its ugly head via the sound, and the way the musical line moves forward (or doesn't) has everything to do with that community.

Some days it is easier for us to get there. On other days, it is a challenge. On those days, the Qigong exercises (detailed earlier in Chapter 2) were the only things that could bring an interior "stability" and calm to our group. Chant teaches us to develop a heightened awareness of others with whom we make music. *It teaches us to respect the musical will of the community and learn from the sounds around us.* We learn to make ourselves less so our sung sound becomes more. In essence, plainchant teaches us that sound truly can be our teacher. It teaches us, ultimately, the deep value of being able to *relax* into the ensemble and *relax* into the sound from that sacred place where grows all things musical. By singing a single line plainchant with others, we can be led to discover a new world of musical expression and musical way of being within the safety and community of others.

Implications Contained in Chanting for Conducting and Teaching

> I learned to value the song for itself, the opposite of theoretical abstraction into key, meter, harmony. Each song created its own world, words, rhythms, pitches, phrases, mood, drama. I learned to stay within that world…. (p. ix)
>
> —Alice Parker
> in *The Answering Voice*

I have spent much time in my professional life pondering the pedagogy of conducting and have tried to make decisions that would lead my students down a more direct path to acquiring both technique and artistry. However, what now seem to be obvious points have somehow eluded me in the past. Plainchant has refreshed my pedagogical screen and prioritized those things that are most important in "allowing" and "guiding." The experience of chant truly empowers us as conductors to be an empathetic initiator and sustainer of sound.

THE VORTEX OF WEIGHT:
THE DILEMMA AND INCARCERATION OF SIGN VERSUS LINE

In both *The Conductor's Gesture* and *Conducting Technique Etudes,* I make the quite emphatic point that one of the major tools in the development of expressive gesture is the mastery both kinesthetically and gesturally of the Laban Efforts in Combination. The mastery of that kinesthetic expressive vocabulary is dependent on one's ability to not only displace weight, but to also withhold weight according to the desired trajectory of any phrase. This presupposes that the conductor has experienced as a performer within an ensemble the kinesthetic of moving sound forward—of what it feels like to move a sound forward in concert with others. Human and musical empathy among and between singers is the key here. *Plainchant has taught me, rather bluntly, that until one experiences musical line as part of a community, one really can only intellectualize about the shape or trajectory of a phrase.* Phrasing can be taught, to be sure, but real learning of phrasing resides within a communal musicing through chant. To be *in* an ensemble sound "envelope" while a line is being sung is quite different from arriving at a phrasing decision based upon notation and singing it in solo. In many ways, we can learn about a phrase easier by going there with others rather than going alone. Going it alone is possible, but exceedingly more difficult. Understanding phrasing and *being in a phrase* is a deeply kinesthetic—and if I may say so, a deeply spiritual—act. We cannot use any gesture to reflect or influence or support musical line unless we have experienced musical line in *communitas*, or within the community that is an ensemble. The kinesthetic of a musical line, its trajectory, and the feeling of being "in a line" can only be experienced, I believe, by performing plainchant within a community. A conductor, armed with interior kinesthetic experiences of singing chant, can then call upon the Laban Efforts in Combination gestures that will empathetically guide the musical line.

Perhaps the most significant lesson that plainchant teaches regarding phrasing is that conductors must understand the vicious vortex that is set up when weight is applied (or not applied) to sound, especially immediately after a barline. Barlines have a more detrimental effect upon musical line than any of us care to admit because, frankly, we do not spend enough time with monophonic music and the early notation systems that somehow intuitively understood that barlines were *not* needed when *ears and community* could guide sound forward! Further, our conducting pedagogy and practice must upload sound first, phrasing first, and additionally what it feels like to perform a phrase in unison within a community.

I must set forth a controversial point here: While one can understand phrasing as a solo singer, that knowledge is not quite the same as musical line experienced in *communitas*. In fact, solo singers might be better served learning the architecture of musical line first through the door of plainchant, rather than solo song. Solo song introduces the barline into the musicing equation! The objective here is to be able to recognize and somewhat "soul-feel" a musical line without the visual weights that modern notation adds. We would do well to understand that our deepest, most intuitive musical kinesthesia regarding line is best informed and learned with as many visual negatives of notation removed from our musical "aural" sightlines. Eye cannot trump ear and line.

Our task as conductors, after experiencing chant, is to acquire a deep and abiding understanding of how to avoid the use of weight when charting the shape and trajectory of a phrase, especially immediately after a barline.[17] We learn to deploy weight only when necessary to affect the acceleration and deceleration of phrases. Our musical GPS of sorts is programmed best, I have found, through the experience of plainchant.

---

17 *The Choral Rehearsal* (GIA) explores the phrasing principles espoused by Marcel Tabuteau, Weston Noble, and Robert Shaw. At the very core of all of these phrasing approaches is the principle of avoidance of weight on musical materials that immediately follow the barline.

History does not repeat it self, but patterns of historical constellations recur. (p. xi)

—Edward Lowinsky
in *Tonality and Atonality*
in *Sixteenth Century Music*

This quote appeared at the very beginning of this book. What we need, first and foremost, to do as conductors and teachers is to approach musical line and phrasing *through and within* the experience of chant. That experience, brought forward, will inform our musicianship and all our musical decisions. There is a type of musical incarceration that music notation creates that can only be avoided by understanding. We must acknowledge that we possess an inbred fear wherein the written vertical barline becomes a type of musical line inhibitor. Ignoring and countering the inhibiting effect of the barline and consciously working against its affects allows all musical lines to achieve a different dimension in forward and arching sound movement. The musical "constellation" that I am hoping reappears is that we will once again return to a deep understanding through sung experience of the natural journey and trajectory that music can and does have if we allow ourselves to be taken on that sound journey. This is not a new journey, but rather one that desperately needs to be re-discovered.

I See Shapes

Chant has taught this author that modern music notation subliminally presents obstacles to both conductor and performer regarding the performance of beautifully shaped and conceived musical line. Through the performance of chant, we begin to learn an intuitive sense of musical line born out of a community singing and moving forward together. Once we have experienced this phrase dynamic, that experience re-shapes our internal kinesthesia on how our body feels when such phrases are being performed. Phrase understandings acquired in this way have the power to "override" our visual senses and bypass the barline tyranny that so many of us experience during rehearsal and performance. When we perform through the experiences of plainchant, we begin to see melodic lines as continuous and uninterrupted shapes with an architecture all their own that has little, if any, relationship to the way musical line is notated. We begin to visualize shapes of melodic line that are a direct result of communal chant experiences. We cannot learn phrasing, ultimately, from the outside in; we can only make the journey from the inside out—and chant is the best vehicle for that journey.

> Freedom is perhaps the ultimate spiritual longing of an individual human being, but freedom is only really appreciated when it falls within the parameters of a larger sense of belonging. (p. 233)
>
> —David Whyte
> in *Crossing the Unknown Sea*

> Axioms in philosophy are not axioms until they have proved upon our pulses; we read fine things but never feel them to the full until we have gone the same steps as the author. (p. 234)
>
> —John Keats in David Whyte,
> *Crossing the Unknown Sea*

AWARENESS OF A MUSICAL ARCH:
THE SONIC PHYSICS OF PLAINCHANT

Music phrasing and influencing, and an ensemble's performance of a phrase, rests with a deep understanding on the part of the conductor upon their concept of the arch of a phrase, or what Wilhelm Ehmann always stressed in my lessons with him, "der grosse bogen"—the big shape of the musical line or, better yet, its trajectory. There are "rules" by which the energy of a line can be cultivated, nurtured, and guided by the conductor. The conductor can only possess that knowledge by understanding the phrasal dynamics, or physics, of chant. Chant teaches us that while musical weight has an expressive value, misapplication of weight interferes with both musical architecture and the trajectory of any phrase.

Interestingly, chant has provided me with clear points at which I must "let go" of the melodic and harmonic textures to achieve a compelling and deeply moving musical arch. Chant should teach us that the biggest musical obstacle to musicianship within our ensembles is the black barline. Similarly, our rhythm notation system, with black notes and beaming, provides a visual handicap and bias to unearthing a musical phrase that is bound to harmonic rhythm in later music. Chant allows us, as conductors, to equip ourselves aurally with an unbiased sound world that is not hampered by notation.

CONCLUSIONS

Our relationship to time has become corrupted exactly because we allow ourselves very little experience of the timeless. We speak continually of saving time, but time in its richness is most often lost to us when we are busy without relief. (p. 176)

—David Whyte
in *Crossing the Unknown Sea*

We have, perhaps for many reasons, bypassed or ignored the very foundation of our "musical DNA" for far too long. Decades of conducting and conducting teaching have created pedagogies that do not do honor or compel us to understand the basic and true elements of what it is to be an artist/musician. Theory has inadvertently trumped intuitive experience, and geometric gesture devoid of internal kinesthetic has perhaps taken over our expressive sensibilities. The way we live our modern lives has caused us to view time in shorter and shorter segments. We somehow as artists have lost the perspective that those who began plainsong understood. That uninterrupted, forward movement of time through sound is the ideal medium for expression. At times, we lose track of the fact that music made by communities of people can inform, uplift, and show us a new and honest route into self-expression that reveals the soul and the meaning of what it is to be human in the world because it compels us to exist in time in the same way...each and every one of us. For me, chant has re-awakened all of the above and has reinforced all those things that I have always believed to be at the core of both ensemble singing and human expression. Plainchant, in its simplicity, forces us to reckon directly with the expressive demons that hold us back and opens to each of us, whether conductor or singer, a newfound way of musical being.

PART II

THE USE AND PURPOSE OF THE CD CONTAINED IN THIS BOOK

James Jordan

Entering into the plainchant with a group of singers is like deciding to take an identical journey together, each step identical, each step simultaneous. Is there anything in music, or life, that even closely resembles this?

I marveled at how lucky I was to learn in this oral tradition, to learn in the way that chant was originally passed down before notation. Imagine the kind of mind it would take to memorize the catalogue of our western liturgical chants? Imagine the dedication of these specialists living and breathing this life in chant!

—Dominic Gregorio from "Living the Chant"
Discovering Chant, pg xxxix

I believe that in this book we have outlined the case for the use of plainchant as an activity that was born out of communal singing. Within that sense of "communitas" is the great unharnessed power of the pedagogy we are proposing here. For many, the performance of chant is deeply intimidating on many levels: from the deciphering of the notation to a stylistic understanding of how to be "musical" with this seemingly foreign sonic world.

Through my work with Edwin Gordon I have realize and understand the value of learning "sound before symbol." For those chained to notation or chained to teaching notation in marriage with sound, this book is trying to move you out of your comfort zone into what may be a different pedagogical path for you—that is, to re-prioritize your teaching away from notation and toward listening, feeling, and being with others in ensemble. My friend and colleague Eugene Migliaro Corporon always says there is a basic principle to being in an ensemble—that is the simple recognition and acceptance that you are in an ensemble. You are part of a larger musical whole, and to be part of that whole you must become part of that communal engagement—part of a listening, feeling community of artists.

To teach and guide the musical concepts in this book, one must be able to model when need be and provide the pedagogical leadership through modeling. This will require a new skills set for many of us. To help you along the way, the CD included with this book will provide the aural "upload" you need to accomplish all of the pedagogical goals presented here. All of the plainchants presented in this book (which have been replicated in an Ensemble Edition), are performed exquisitely by Isabella Burns.

The process for using the CD is as follows:

1. **Listen repeatedly to the CD.** Listen to the CD many, many times without singing or looking at the notation. In the Music Learning Theory world, this is called the aural/oral level of learning. This is the most important step in any music learning process. Sound before sight. Sound before notation. If you do not spend enough time within this level of learning, you might experience a frustration when moving to chant notation.

2. **After repeated listening, listen to the CD while looking at the notation, but do not sing.** This level of association is a necessary step. By having the aural model "in your ear," you will be able to bring meaning to notation rather than trying to derive meaning from notation when a strong aural image is not present in your audiation. Listen again to a particular chant repeated times, but *do not sing.*

3. **Listen to the CD again; this time, look at the notated chant and move your hand and body to the chant.** One of the important, perhaps crucial, musical understandings you will gain using chant is a new way of moving music forward. The experience of sound moving forward is a deeply kinesthetic one. To learn the "style" of chant, you must become vested to how it moves forward. This can only be learned in a way that counteracts previous "bad" habits by experiencing through your own body how it feels to be immersed in the forward movement of chant.

4. **Listen to the chant and breathe and exhale in empathy with the sung chant you are hearing.** It is important to learn the breath necessary to sing chant as a separate process at first. Exhalation while listing to the chant will internalize the forward movement of the chant through breath energy. This breath process is a necessary process.[18]

5. **Begin to sing the chant using the neutral syllable "noo."** Now you are ready to begin singing chant. Find your starting pitch, as instructed on the CD, and begin singing. If at first you have trouble, isolate and perform only portions of the chant. This is akin to learning to speak phrases before you speak sentences. (To those familiar with Music Learning Theory, this is known as the Partial Synthesis level of music learning.) *Make sure the breath taken prior to singing is energized!*

6. **Add text.** Sing the chants as notated with text. From time to time, add hand movement to reinforce forward movement without weight.

Author's Note: For those of you who are teachers reading this book, you have probably already realized that one of the great rewards of teaching is being taught by your students. Isabella Burns, a Westminster Choir College undergraduate student, has sung chant for most of her life. Her musicianship and deep commitment to chant has inspired all of us. She has been my teacher in learning all things chant. Hers is the voice you hear on the CD. Without her, this journey would have been more difficult than the joy it has been for all of us.

---

18 For those who wish to explore this concept of breathing with energy and spirit, you are strongly encouraged to read and study *The Musician's Breath* (GIA).

CD TRACK LISTING

Track

1   Two Alleluias

2   Surrexit Dominus

3   Agnus Dei

4   Psalm 121

5   Psalm 150

6   Tantum Ergo

7   Veni Creator

8   Call to Remembrance

9   Kyrie Eleison

10   Ave Maria

11   Salve Regina

12   Elegerunt Apostoli Stephanum

13–23 Compline

24   Instructions for Finding Notes

LAUDATE
ESSENTIAL CHANTS FOR ALL MUSICIANS

LAUDATE

ESSENTIAL CHANTS FOR ALL MUSICIANS

SELECTED AND EDITED BY
JAMES WHITBOURN

WITH A PERFORMANCE COMMENTARY BY
ISABELLA BURNS

CHANT ENGRAVINGS BY CORTLANDT MATTHEWS

THE COMPANION COLLECTION TO JAMES JORDAN'S
DISCOVERING CHANT

COMPANION MP3 DOWNLOADS OF THE CHANTS
CONTAINED IN THIS VOLUME AVAILABLE AT
WWW.GIAMUSIC.COM/LAUDATE

GIA PUBLICATIONS, INC.
CHICAGO

Dedicated to the

CHORAL INSTITUTE AT OXFORD,

its resident choir, the

WESTMINSTER WILLIAMSON VOICES,

and in memory of

DR. MARY BERRY

(1917-2008)

leader, innovator, and educator

in the re-discovery of chant

Laudate
Essential Chants for All Musicians

James Whitbourn

G-8812A
ISBN: 978-1-62277-121-9

Copyright © 2014 GIA Publications, Inc.
7404 S. Mason Ave
Chicago IL 60638

GIA Publications, Inc.
www.giamusic.com

All rights reserved.
Printed in the United States of America.

Art direction/design: Martha Chlipala
Engravings: Cortlandt Matthews

TABLE OF CONTENTS

COMMENTARY FOR PERFORMERS

A set of performance notes to each chant (shown in boxes) have been prepared by Isabella

Burns. Ideally, students should read them in conjunction with her recordings of the chants.

This can be accessed via the website www.giamusic.com/laudate.

FOREWORD

James Jordan

Chant allows us to be alone but with others; chant asks us to make ourselves less so others become more; it asks us to serve something larger than ourselves and demands of us to listen deeply so we always hear what is best in ourselves. Chant creates a sacred place for communities of singers unlike anything else I know or have ever experienced.

Because of its sonic bare bones, chant leaves us a bit vulnerable to elements of pitch, rhythm, and intonation, and forces us to breathe with others, to enter into musical community, and to be carried by our ears as we sing. For those who are courageous, the singing of their ensembles will go beyond what they could have ever imagined. And because of that, it is worth the risk.

This collection provides a wealth of material for developing your musicianship in many dimensions. Singing these chants in ensemble builds ensemble musicianship, intonation, a strong sense of interior rhythm and, above all, a natural and deeply intuitive way of phrasing. These chants form a musical diet by which musicianship can grow in many ways. The companion text, *Discovering Chant* (GIA), provides conductors and all those interested with detailed explanations regarding the philosophy and pedagogical importance of this material.

I recommend that at the end of the vocal or technical choral warm-up for each rehearsal, five to ten minutes be spent focusing on chant. Starting the rehearsal in such a way will bring both ears and spirits into the place necessary for the rehearsal to come.

5

WHY SINGING PLAINCHANT MATTERS: AN INTRODUCTION

THE LEGACY OF AN INSPIRATIONAL EDUCATOR

A small advertisement placed in one of the British newspapers early in 1979 set me on a journey that would influence my whole musical life. The notice, placed in the personal column, advertised a plainchant course at Girton College, Cambridge, run by Dr. Mary Berry and her Schola Gregoriana of Cambridge, which she had formed just four years earlier. My mother saw the notice and passed it to me. I was fifteen years old at the time and had already developed a strong interest in medieval and early music. Supported by my parents, I enrolled in the course. I can still remember arriving in Cambridge for that course—slightly out of place, it must be said, as a fifteen-year-old. Everyone else was much older; they were already clutching their copies of the *Liber Usualis*,[1] a volume hitherto unknown to me. Thus began my journey of discovery in this extraordinary repertoire, which I followed throughout the following decades. After the Girton course, I quickly signed up for the next one, at Queens' College, Cambridge, the following January, and later became one of the group of singers that Mary Berry called her Schola Gregoriana of Cambridge. With her and the other singers, I traveled to many parts of Europe taking my part in some extraordinary projects, all led with a burning passion that cannot easily be replicated (and in England, has probably not been seen since Mary's death in 2008).

For Mary Berry, plainchant was her life, and no detail was too small to be of interest. Although she was vowed to a religious life (and remained Mother Thomas More), she was an extraordinary evangelist for the chant, encouraging as many people as possible to hold onto the enormous musical heritage that had been all but discarded by the Second Vatican Council. As Fellow and Director of Studies at Newham College, Cambridge, she was a recognized scholar who continued to delve and discover, and to experiment.

---

1   *Liber Usualis,* edited by the Benedictines of Solesmes, France, and printed in Belgium. There were various editions, including editions with English rubrics from 1934.

6

It was on one of her experimental weekends that I remember most strongly being struck by the power of chant. Mary had invited a small group of us to spend the weekend at her home singing through new chants she had found and trying out some new theories of rhythm. Her rehearsal technique was best suited to small groups and relied heavily on repetition and intense listening. These were the days long before mobile phones, so checking e-mails and other similar distractions that confront contemporary musicians today did not exist. The atmosphere was intense, serious, and focused. It was, however, hard. It was hard because the rhythmic aspect of the chant was difficult to notate and had to be felt, understood, and agreed by the singers. After many hours of rehearsal, a miracle occurred. We started to sing the chants almost perfectly together. It was the most perfect unison I had ever experienced or have experienced since, and I recall a feeling of exhilaration at our having achieved it. It may seem like a strange source of exhilaration—and maybe it was one of those "you had to be there" moments—but the feeling of singing complex chant in exact unison brought about a palpable feeling of unity among those of us who took part. It was a more intense experience than any polyphonic performance I have witnessed because each of us was listening to and feeling so profoundly what the other musicians were doing, and if anyone should fall out of unison, it would be immediately apparent. It brought about a unity of musical thought and a shared understanding of musical phrase, shape, and direction.

Journeys with Mary Berry also led me to some spectacular auditory experiences that made me understand the true nature of this music. The best of these were the visits to the Abbey at Pontigny in France, easily the most beautiful natural acoustic I have heard. Not only is the decay enormously long (about twelve seconds), it is also beautiful, clean, and uncluttered. Somehow the walls of this particular building are constructed in the perfect material and shape to create an echo chamber that illuminates the polyphonic nature of chant in unimaginable ways. I should explain that remark, since a reference to the polyphonic nature of a monophonic piece of music may seem contradictory.

7

Early in the twenty-first century, many composers have adopted a technique of using chord "clusters," meaning chords that contain simultaneous seconds and thirds that cling to the dominant notes of the chord, giving them new resonances. A single unison line sung in Pontigny Abbey, though, gives that effect and more without the intervention of a composer, as all the notes sung in the previous ten to twelve seconds continue to sound on. In many ways, the chord cluster is a compositional device developed for dry buildings, which apes a sonority that has been known for hundreds of years—and is almost taken for granted—by those who sing in big, reverberant buildings. Interestingly, I attended parish worship one morning in Pontigny, where a small instrumental music group accompanied the worship. How this contrasted with the intensely beautiful lines of the plainsong I had heard the previous day. The building's monumental reverberation served as acoustic confusion as sounds fought and shattered each other's harmonics into sonic chaos. It is a building that cannot cope with polyphony (other than that which it creates itself), but which is revelatory in the monophonic repertory.

Many of Mary Berry's "away" workshops focused on particular liturgical reconstructions, usually of the places in which we were singing. I remember one in particular, at which we undertook the entire cycle of Daily Offices, requiring us to get up in the middle of the night at three-hour intervals to continue the recitation of the psalms. Painful though this felt at the time, it engendered in all of us who took part a sense of the familiarity of the chants that monastic communities would have felt, but so much more strongly than we did. If, even after a few days of singing this way, we developed an understanding of timing and nuance in our singing, we could imagine how this would have developed in a lifetime.

THE POWER OF CHANT IN THE DEVELOPMENT OF MUSICIANS

The immersion in plainchant had a deeper effect on my musical development than I realized at the time. By working with the chant, I came to love the fluidity of a musical melodic phrase and an expression of words through musical ornament. I

8

also came to recognize the freedom that was obtainable without the constriction of bar lines or the temporal limitations of polyphony. In particular, I came to recognize the benefits of a notational system that could reflect the fluidity of the music in its visual manifestation. This was most noticeably the case when we worked from the earliest notational systems that did not use staffs or pitched notes at all.[2] But even within the conventional plainsong four-line staff and square note heads (as used in this book), it is easy to see the shape of the phrase.

In some ways, though, I always remained a foreigner. Unlike Mary Berry, I had not decided to devote my whole life to the chant: I had many other musical interests and it merely took its place among them. But the chance to work with a world expert on the repertory presented an opportunity that I value highly. The occasions today when I regularly sing the chant are relatively few, and even then they tend to be the more basic chants rather than the highly decorated and florid chants that really made their impact upon me. But in spite of that, I regard plainchant as one of the fundamentals of my musicianship.

It is the fundamental nature of plainchant that makes it important for all who practice music in the tradition of the Western musical world. Even a cursory glance will reveal the fundamentality of plainchant throughout the corpus of European sacred music of the renaissance and beyond. This is clear to see in the vast repertory of polyphonic masses based on a plainchant *cantus firmus,* for example, and the melismatic[3] nature of line that permeates all of renaissance polyphony. But there are some more surprising examples of the fundamentality of chant.

---

2   This early system of notation consisted of small line strokes written above the text, which indicated a rise or fall in pitch but did not specify the exact interval. The notation was used to aid the memory of a singer who had already learned the chant through aural repetition. Despite its inexact pitch definitions, the notational system is surprisingly detailed and contains much important information about early performance practice.

3   A melisma indicates the singing of a single syllable to more than one note. Melismatic chants are accordingly more florid than syllabic chants, where notes are arranged one per syllable.

9

THE ESSENCE OF CHANT IN THE CONCERT HALL AND OPERA HOUSE

In 2013, St Stephen's House, Oxford, hosted the inaugural Choral Institute at Oxford in collaboration with Westminster Choir College. This was also the hundredth anniversary of the birth of Benjamin Britten, in recognition of which we decided to make Britten one of our featured composers for the course. Being born in 1913, Britten was brought up and educated in a pre-Vatican II world. Further, hymnbooks in Britain at that time—such as the *English Hymnal*—included a number of plainsong hymns. Those hymns would have been known and sung in schools from time to time, and those he heard obviously stuck in his mind. In his compositions, Britten uses plainsong explicitly on several occasions. One obvious example comes at the beginning and closing of *A Ceremony of Carols*,[4] which uses the plainsong antiphon *Hodie Christus natus est*.[5] Other explicit examples are the use of *Te lucis ante terminum*[6] in *Curlew River*[7] and *Nunc dimittis*[8] in *St. Nicolas*.[9] The *St. Nicolas* example is the most decorated of these examples in that it is woven into the tapestry of the score, but essentially these are all extant plainchant melodies or tones quoted within an otherwise original work. These examples all indicate an easy familiarity with plainchant, which I believe also finds its way into Britten's work in less explicit ways. Consider, for example, the cantation of Nicolas in Movement V of *St. Nicolas*. This example shows that easy familiarity almost as clearly as the explicit quotations. It has that recognizable characteristic of a monotonic recitation gently shaped with rising notes and then provided with a florid, melismatic chant-like ending.

---

4   *A Ceremony of Carols*, Boosey & Hawkes, 1942.
5   Antiphon to *Magnificat* at Second Vespers, Christmas Day; *Liber Usualis*, 1952, p. 413.
6   Benjamin Britten wrote in his program notes, "I have started the work with that wonderful plainsong hymn 'Te lucis ante terminum' and from it the whole piece may be said to have grown." Program note to the 1964 Aldeburgh Festival performance, quoted by W. Anthony Sheppard in *Revealing Masks*, University of California Press, p. 127.
7   Benjamin Britten *Curlew River*, Faber Music Ltd., 1964.
8   The choir sings the English translation of the Nunc Dimittis from the 1662 Book of Common Prayer in Movement 9 of *St. Nicolas*, beginning at Figure 61 (Boosey & Hawkes 1948 edition). It is set to Tone IV, ending 4, as set out in *A Manual of Plainsong for Divine Service*, edited by H. B. Briggs and W. H. Frere, Novello & Co, 1969.
9   Benjamin Britten, *St. Nicolas*, Boosey & Hawkes, 1948.

10

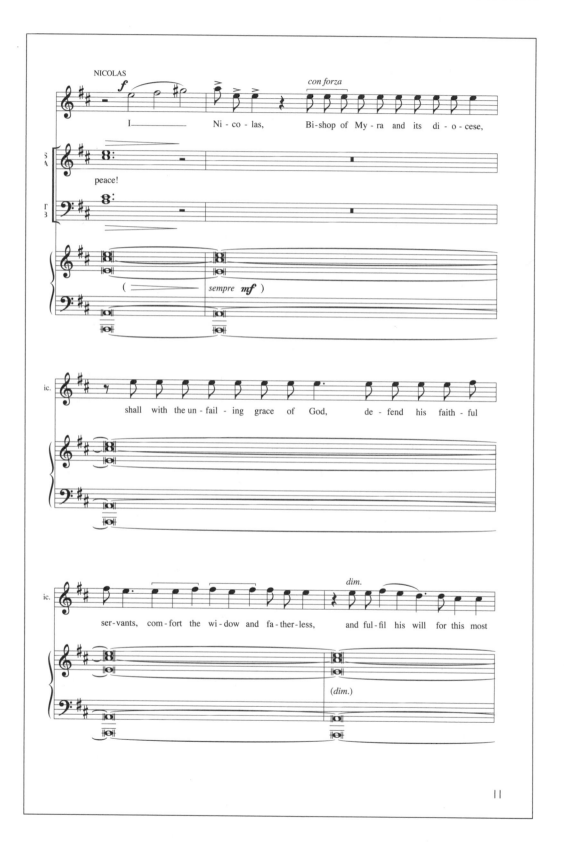

Then consider Britten's final opera *Death in Venice:*[10] his recitative, though not adopting the modality of medieval plainchant, assumes its very essence and highlights the true nature of plainchant to the contemporary musician in a way that is perhaps more direct than looking at the medieval examples. Britten's purpose is to serve the words and to give them greater distinctiveness through the defining of pitch. The words themselves inject the melody with rhythm, just as happens in plainchant, rather than having rhythm imposed upon them by the bar line-based notation of more recent centuries. Here, Britten even uses the convention used in modern transcriptions of plainchant of writing in stemless note heads.

These twentieth-century examples of monophony can be surprisingly illuminating when projected back to their medieval ancestors, because through them we can understand more of the *essence* of the musical intention. We know that Britten used this technique not because he wished to pay homage to some historical antiquity, but because he believed chant-like monophony to be the most direct and effective way of communicating a set of words, critical to the story he tells. Nor should the significance of this being his final opera be overlooked: this was no youthful compositional attempt, but the work of a composer whose craft was fully developed to the highest levels and whose musical language was complete.

10   Benjamin Britten, *Death in Venice*, Faber Music Ltd., 1973.

12

To me, these successors to plainchant make the importance of the original repertoire even greater. In the middle of the twentieth century, traditional plainchant frequently suffered in the hands of poor and turgid performances. The monastic imperative had been replaced by a waning attempt to cling onto a museum piece, the provenance of which was not fully understood. It was often accompanied (and often poorly) on the organ—further detracting from the vocal essence of the repertoire. So Mary Berry's passion was a shining beacon for the authentic musicality of plainchant. But so, too, was Britten's modern-day adaptation, shining the spotlight onto the beauty of monophony when presented without rhythmic device and when left to form a natural phrase.

CHANT REDISCOVERED FOR MODERN MUSICIANS

My journeys working with James Jordan and Westminster Choir College brought me to a new realization in 2011 when working on a recording project. Within the project we were to record a work of mine for saxophone and organ, *A brief story of Peter Abelard,*[11] a set of variations on the plainchant melody by Peter Abelard,[12] *O quanta qualia*. Each of the variations portrays an episode in the remarkable life of Abelard, and it uses the hymn I had first sung in Pontigny Abbey some years earlier. For the recording, I asked the choir to sing the plainchant hymn as a prelude to the instrumental piece. I imagined that this would be a moment's work and would be the most straightforward item on the list. The Williamson Voices is one of Westminster Choir College's elite chamber choirs and is a highly accomplished and polished choir. On the recording list were several taxing items, all performed with precision and poise. But when it came to the simple plainchant hymn, the choir struggled to find a convincing style. The style required was new to everyone, it seemed. In the end, we decided to abandon the idea and leave the instrumental piece to stand alone. It

---

11   James Whitbourn, *A brief story of Peter Abelard*, Chester Music, 2006, originally for alto saxophone and piano. Re-scored for soprano saxophone and organ in 2011.

12   Peter Abelard was a twelfth-century French scholar whose love affair with his pupil Héloïse became one of the most celebrated love stories.

14

was at this point that I understood the depth of neglect that plainchant had suffered, even in high-level music colleges, and James Jordan and I discussed this at length at that time. When, two years later, we had the chance to start our Choral Institute at Oxford, we placed chant high on the agenda.

The first introduction to plainchant the students of the Choral Institute received came just hours after they arrived in Oxford, when I took them through a whistle-stop tour of semiology, square notation, and liturgy. I asked the fifty-strong choir how many people had covered this ground before and just one hand went up (that of Isabella Burns who has helped me with this collection and who, after our first Institute, worked with James Jordan and his choir to re-discover the chant with such spectacular results).

During that first introduction, most people—in their jet-lagged state—were unaware of the significance of the building in which they sat and its relevance to the subject matter at hand. St Stephen's House occupies the former monastic buildings of the Society of St. John the Evangelist or the "Cowley Fathers" as they are commonly known. It is a building that sits as one of the visible manifestations of the Oxford Movement—the nineteenth-century movement associated with the University of Oxford—which eventually sought to reclaim the medieval roots of English Christianity in every aspect and which developed into the churchmanship known as High Anglicanism or Anglo-Catholicism. The ideals of the leaders of the Oxford Movement expanded to the rediscovery of the rich heritage of devotional and spiritual life that had been lost or obscured in the post-Reformation Church. By stretching back to pre-Reformation religious life, those who joined the Oxford Movement returned to the Roman Catholic roots of the Anglican (Episcopalian) Church, both in their internal spiritual life and in its outward, invisible manifestations. They re-evaluated the strengths of gothic architecture, re-examined liturgical practice (now with the Eucharist at its heart), and started to unearth the musical riches that had been wholly or partially lost, but with a view to applying to it an Anglican slant. The buildings now occupied by St Stephen's House represent an important stage in the history of the Oxford Movement: they were built to house a whole monastic

15

community. Here, then, was the construction of a new monastery—the model of religious community at the very heart of the program of destruction set out at the Reformation (the Dissolution of the Monasteries)—but now built to a new, Anglican model. In Britain we have a phrase to say that someone "throws out the baby with the bath water." The leaders of the Oxford Movement believed that indeed the baby had been thrown out with the bath water, but that it was not too late to save it.

Among the lost heritage of the Church in England was the vast corpus of plainchant used in medieval times, associated with Salisbury Cathedral. The so-called "Sarum" use (Sarum being the ancient name for Salisbury) recognized Salisbury Cathedral as being the leader of its day, though liturgical practices developed for local use in Salisbury had spread to other parts of England and beyond. The short introit in this collection, *Call to remembrance*, is taken from a volume of introits[13] published in 1918 by St. Mary's Convent, Wantage (a religious community close to Oxford), of music adapted from the *Sarum Gradale* by the Rev. G. H. Palmer. Palmer and Francis Burgess were two of the leading figures responsible for re-introducing plainchant melodies, albeit by matching them to the vernacular rather than the Latin texts. Notwithstanding the shortcomings of these chants, with their sometimes-stilted English texts, the work of Palmer and Burgess was a crucial step back to the corpus of music that formed the basis of so much of the Western music we know.

OPENING CHANT TO ALL MUSICIANS

This volume similarly aims to provide a stepping stone. It is a primer for those who are new to the chant but who see how necessary it is to understand this vast and influential repertoire. It is also a primer that recognizes that many obstacles currently stand in the way of the curious browser.

One of the obstacles is that few have regular access to plainchant in its proper liturgical form. In its most authentic form the repertoire of medieval chant is part of a life of total commitment and devotion. Even a few days spent in this way gives

---

13   *The Offices, or Introits, for Sunday and Festivals with musical notation from The Sarum Gradale*, adapted by the Rev. G. H. Palmer, St. Mary's Convent, Wantage, 1918.

16

a glimpse into a different mindset in which the passing of time is marked by the sounding of the Daily Office and the progression of liturgical seasons. A short exposure to it also teaches how some of the chants quickly become second nature, how swiftly the ability to listen intensifies, and how ensemble binds. Few are called permanently to this level of religious devotion and yet the music that stems from it needs to become part of the skill set of everyone who wishes to acquire the fullest understanding of choral music.

Secondly, four-line staff, square-note notation is unfamiliar to most modern musicians. Most would agree that after a little practice the system of notation proves a far easier and far more effective system than a modern transcription allows; but it takes a little work to get into it. On this point, I would urge everyone to persevere. In my experience, the hardest thing about singing from traditional square notation is the sounding of the first few notes—getting the sense of tonality and working out the first few intervals. In that sense, the cantor's job is usually the hardest as the solo voice that sets the tonality and the speed. In this volume, while generally sticking with square notation, we have provided a transcription of the first few notes of each piece into modern notation, intended as a helpful way to get started.

Thirdly, there is the question of language. It is hard, sometimes, when grappling with a new system of notation to be simultaneously reading at speed an unfamiliar Latin text. We have tried to help by providing some chants early in the collection that have familiar or simple texts or that have an English text. After all, the chanting of psalms, for example, is just as effective in English, and mastering this is an excellent way to get started with psalmody. It means that singers should be able to concentrate better on the new notation and on the sounds that they are making while having to glance only briefly at the text.

There are other obstacles too: many plainchant collections contain a large amount of specialist liturgical terminology, and there are notational short-forms that are unique to square-note notation. In some volumes, the explanatory notes themselves are written in Latin, making it difficult for most newcomers to understand. This

17

collection aims to dispense with as many of these obstacles as possible, not because they are unnecessary but simply because they prevent many people even getting to the starting line.

Perhaps the greatest center for the restoration and organization of vast quantities of the plainchant repertory in post-medieval times has been the Abbey of Solesmes in France, whose monks created a monumental volume of chants (almost two thousand pages of them) all carefully and intricately arranged for liturgical use. Their *Liber Usualis*, first published at the end of the nineteenth century and then revised and expanded through the twentieth, has been the most influential collection and remains an essential companion for scholars and practitioners of the chant. The work, currently available in online versions, has made an extraordinary impact on the understanding of the long-standing importance of the monophonic, freely rhythmic vocal music that has dominated Western music for so many centuries.

But in spite of the work of Solesmes, the leaders of the Oxford Movement, and many others, plainchant remains a repertory that is in perilous danger of being forgotten about again and treated once more as an historical and antiquated art form. So, above all, this volume is designed to be practical. It is designed to place a small collection of chants into the hands of people who will sing them. Through singing them and practicing them together, I hope singers will discover for themselves the intense beauty that is available to them in this simple, yet sophisticated music. By paring choral music down to its very essence, I hope the layers that have built up over many years can be cleaned away and the gems that are to be found in this music can shine through. And I hope that those who have discovered a little will go in search of more, because there is an almost un-minable quantity to be found. One way or another, this is music that choral musicians have to know and understand just as a writer has to know the alphabet. Those who seek to discover will find themselves well rewarded.

18

READING PLAINCHANT IN SQUARE NOTATION

It is not hard to read plainchant in its traditional square notation. In this section, we outline the essential points you need to get started. Throughout this text we have included some additional tips (in sans serif font and boxed) written by Isabella Burns, based on her experience of teaching plainchant to a choir previously unfamiliar with chant singing.

Plainchant is written on a four-line staff (rather than a five-line staff) since most plainchant melodies fit within the range of a ninth. When they exceed the range, the staff is extended for the notes that require this in exactly the same way the ledger line augments a five-line staff.

The note heads are all black in color, are of a square shape, and are without stems. When the music is syllabic (meaning one note is allocated to each syllable of the text), the notation always appears in this simple form.

A few variants occur when the music contains instances where more than one note is sung to a single syllable of the text (known as *melismatic style*). In those cases, the note heads are grouped together to form special notational symbols, most of which occurred through the original method of writing by hand with a quill pen. They can all be readily understood in that context. Once you get used to these note groups, you will find they are easier to read than if the notes had been separated because you can see more easily how each note relates to those around it.

SPECIAL SYMBOLS

Sometimes you will find instances where one note is written directly above the other. This does not indicate a sudden moment of polyphony, nor does it indicate alternative options. Both notes are sung, but one after the other, with the lower notes

19

always sung first. Again, this is a convention derived from early handwritten notation probably retained to save space and therefore fit more music onto a valuable piece of parchment.

Short stems that sometimes occur (usually on the left of a note or joining notes together) are similar conventions derived from handwritten notation as the pen moves up and down the page making a thin line. They have no rhythmic significance.

We occasionally find diamond-shaped note heads, typically in descending passages. It is easy to see how these diamond shapes occurred, as a scribe would hold the quill at a different angle for descending notes. There is no musical difference from the square notes, though. The convention has been retained, however, even in the days of modern printing, since the original diamond shapes of the handwritten notes tend to show the contour of the phrase well and are thought to be helpful to the singers.

Rhythm in plainchant is generated from within the musical phrase and becomes apparent only when the music is learned. In notational terms, rhythm is rarely indicated. The only common exceptions are a dot after the note (which doubles its length) and a line above a set of notes (which indicates a temporary slowing).

A further scribe-based notational convention occurs sometimes when there is a sequence of notes high-low-high. You will see a solid line between the high and low notes that looks as though it may be a glissando. It is not a glissando; just sing the high pitch and the low pitch, and nothing in between.

There are two other cases that require special mention: a tooth-edged note (called a *quilisma*) and a small note usually on a soft consonant (called a *liquiscent*). The quilisma indicates a special pushing through the note in a forward direction. It is somewhat like a crescendo with a rubato lengthening on the note before it.

The liquescent is a "liquid" sound—a type of humming. It occurs on soft consonants, such as "l" and "n," and provides a beautiful smoothing of the text in performance.

One piece of notation that is designed to help singers is a small note-like symbol at the end of each staff. This is a guide that shows the pitch of the first note of the next line. Remember not to sing the guide note!

21

Vertical strokes are used in scores—sometimes short and sometimes across the full staff—and they look rather like bar lines. They are used as punctuation points and are helpful in performance, but they do not have rhythmic implications as bar lines do.

GETTING STARTED

The hardest thing in reading plainchant is getting hold of the tonality of the piece and singing the first few notes. Once that is settled, everything else falls into place quite easily. Plainchant is not notated at any particular pitch: it is assumed that the singers will find a pitch that suits the range of their voices. It is a good idea to look at the highest point and the lowest point and use that to guide your starting pitch. You need to work out where the semitones (half steps) lie; there will be a clef to help you do this. The most common clef is the "C" clef. There is also an "F" clef. Either clef shows you the position of the relevant semitone (below the line on which the clef sits).

Don't worry if you find you cannot read the chant right away. Even experienced singers often need to take a moment to work out the first few notes. Take a few moments to work out how the first few notes relate to the semitone shown in the clef. To help you get started, we have included a transcription of the first few notes of each piece onto a modern staff at suggested pitches. If you find you don't need these and can work it out for yourself, then so much the better!

FINDING PITCHES WITH SOLFEGE

A good way to find the starting note and establish the tonality is to use solfege. First, find the note that sits on the clef (in this collection always the "Do" clef). Start on that note as "Do" and sing down the major scale—counting the lines and spaces just as you would with a five-line staff—until you reach the starting pitch of the chant. Perhaps the best way to learn this technique is to listen to the downloadable

22

5 PSALM 150 (CONT.)

TRACK 5

CHOIR 2

CHOIR 1

6. Ré-qui-em ae - tér - nam dó-na é-is Dó-mi-ne.   7. Et lux per-pé-tu-a   lú-ce-at é-is

FULL

Óm-nis spí-ri-tus   láu-det Dó-mi-num.

35

6 TANTUM ERGO

The words of *Tantum ergo* form the last two verses of a longer hymn, *Pange lingua gloriosi mysterium* (sometimes sung in the English version "Of the glorious body telling"), written by the thirteenth-century theologian and philosopher St. Thomas Aquinas. These final two verses have become a hymn in their own right. *Tantum ergo* is especially associated with the service of Benediction (sometimes used as a conclusion to the service of Compline) when the Blessed Sacrament is solemnly exposed to public view in a vessel, surrounded by lights, and to the accompaniment of hymns and prayers. The text has been set to music many times by composers such as Fauré and Schubert. Many choral directors will already be familiar with the plainchant setting through the beautiful harmonization made by Duruflé—one of his set of *Quatre Motets sur des thèmes grégoriens*.

I suggest practicing the melody on solfège until the choir is comfortable with it, then adding the text back in. If the choir is large enough, it may not be necessary to break at the quarter bar. This point can be left to the discretion of the choir director. As with all chant—though particularly with hymns and chants of a repetitive nature—no weight should be added onto the ends of phrases or descending intervals. These notes should be tapered and placed with care.

TRANSLATION

Accordingly, bowing down, let us worship so great a Sacrament; let the Old Law give way to the new rite: let faith furnish reinforcement for what our senses fail to perceive.

To the Begetter [Father] and to the Begotten [Son] be praise and jubilation, as well as salvation, honor, power, and blessing: to the One [Spirit] proceeding from both be equal praise.

36

6 TANTUM ERGO

TRACK 6

SOLO   FULL

Tán-tum ér-go Sac-ra-mén-tum   Ve-ne-ré-mur cér-nu-i: Et an-tí-quum do-cu-mén-tum

Nó-vo cé-dat rí-tu-i;   Praé-stet fí-des sup-ple-mén-tum Sén-su-um de-féc-tu-i.

Ge-ni-tó-ri,   Ge-ni-tó-que Laus et ju-bi-lá-ti-o,   Sá-lus, hó-nor, vír-tus quó-que

Sit et be-ne-dí-cti-o;   Pro-ce-dén-ti ab ut-ró-que Cóm-par sit lau-dá-ti-o.   Á-men.

7 VENI CREATOR

One of the plainchant repertory's most famous hymns, *Veni Creator,* is thought to have been written in the ninth century. It is frequently sung at Pentecost and at the ordination of priests and bishops. In many liturgical books, hymns are presented with the words detached from the melody, and it can sometimes be difficult to fit the words together in performance, especially if Latin is unfamiliar. This often has the effect of slowing down the music while people concentrate on the mechanics of reading music and words from different parts of the page. In this collection, we have written all the words under the music so it is easy to read. This should allow singers to concentrate on the shape and line of the melody and to feel its natural rhythm. *Veni Creator* needs to be sung with a flowing style—not too slowly—while enjoying the interesting patterns of note groups. This way, the true beauty of these ancient melodies will emerge.

| Do | ti | la | so | So | la | so | fa | so | la | so | do | re | do |
| Ve | - ni | cre | - | - | a | - tor—— | | | Spi | - ri | - tu |

As with "Tantum ergo," first familiarize the choir with the melody via solfège. With chants of this length, if at all possible, split the choir into two parts and alternate verses between the two groups. This way, it is not so tiring on the voice and adds an element of variation. There are some instances in this piece where the Latin text has been compressed so it fits the meter of the melody. In verse 3, "digitus" becomes "digtus" (the "g" remains soft). In verse 4, "infunde" becomes "infund" and elides with the next word "amorem." There are other versions where instead of changing the text, the meter is broken by adding an extra note to accommodate the text, such as "perpetui" instead of "perpeti."

Translation

Come, creator Spirit, visit these souls of yours:
Fill with heavenly grace the hearts which you have created.

1. Come, creator Spirit, visit these souls of yours: Fill with heavenly grace the hearts that you have created,

2. You who are called Paraclete [Advocate], gift of God most high, fount of life, of fire, of love, and spiritual anointing.

3. You are sevenfold in gifts, the [fore]finger of the Father's right hand, you are duly promised by the Father, empowering our throats with speech.

38

7 VENI CREATOR

TRACK 7

SOLO   FULL

1. Ve - ni, Cre - á - tor Spí - ri - tus, Men - tes tu - ó - rum ví - si - ta: Im-ple su - pér - na

grá - ti - a Quae tu cre - ás - ti, pé-cto-ra. 2. Qui dí - ce - ris Pa - rá - cli - tus, Al - tís - si-

-mi dó - num Dé - i, Fons ví - vus, íg - nis, ca - ri - tas, Et spi - ri - tá - lis ún - cti - o.

3. Tu sep - ti - fór - mis mú - ne - re, Díg-tus pa - tér - nae déx - ter - ae, Tu ri - te pro - mís-

- sum Pá - tris Ser-mó - ne dí - tans gút - tu - ra. 4. Ac - cén - de lú - men sén - si - bus, In - fúnd

a - mó - rem cór - di - bus, In - fír - ma no - stri cór - po - ris, Vir - tú - te fír - mans pér - pe - ti.

TRANSLATION (CONT.)

4. Kindle light in our thoughts [enlighten our minds], instill love in our hearts,
   strengthening by your perpetual power the weakness of our bodies.

5. May you drive the enemy further away, and grant us everlasting peace. So,
   with you as leader guiding us, we may avoid all harm.

6. Grant that through you, we may know the Father, and be acquainted with
   the Son, (and) you, Spirit of them both, may we trust for all time.

39

7 VENI CREATOR (CONT.)

TRACK 7

5. Hó-stem re-pél-las lón-gi-us, Pa-cém-que dó-nes pró-ti-nus: Du-ctó-re sic te

práe-vi-o, Vi-te-mus óm-ne nó-xi-um. 6. Per te sci-á-mus da Pá-trem, No-scá-mus

at-que Fí-li-um, Te ut-ri-ús-que Spí-ri-tum Cre-dá-mus óm-ni tém-po-re.

A - men.

40

8 CALL TO REMEMBRANCE

For many centuries, a huge repertory of plainchant was lost outside the Roman Catholic Church until a small group of scholars and musicians started to re-discover it at the middle of the nineteeth century. The musical archaeologists centered on the city and university of Oxford and were part of what became known as "The Oxford Movement." A leading figure in the re-discovery of plainchant was G. H. Palmer (1846–1926), who published many collections of chants adapted for Anglican (Episcopalian) use with English translations fitted to the original melodies. Palmer directed the music for a time at the Church of St. John the Evangelist, now part of St. Stephen's House, Oxford, where there is a plaque dedicated to his memory. *Call to Remembrance* comes from a collection of introits published in 1918 through St. Mary's Convent, Wantage, with music from the Sarum Gradale. It is set for the second Sunday in Lent. Singing chant with English translations can allow singers to learn chants more readily since the underlay can be easily assimilated, and can help acquire freedom of line and shape.

The melodic aspect of this piece is quite simple, though beautiful. The musical phrasing should follow the natural phrases of the text. There are several instances in this piece that utilize the liquescent (see page 21). As with Latin, the consonants are voiced on the little note, "m" in remembrance, and "n" in both "against" and "unto." Here we see some instances of a high-low-high (called a "porrectus"). The appearance of this neum comes from the old practice of dragging a calligraphy pen across the page, presumably to save time when writing. When singing a high-low-high (such as the syllable "mer" of "mercy"), it is important to note that even though the long bar may span across more than three notes, only three are sung: the line or space where the neum begins, the point it touches at the bottom, and the point where it rests at the end.

41

8 CALL TO REMEMBRANCE

TRACK 8

SOLO   FULL

Call to re-mem-brance   thy ten-der com-pas-sion   and mer-cy,   O Lord, and thy

lov-ing kind-nes-ses to-wards us, which have been ev-er of old: nei-ther suf-fer our

e-ne-mies to tri-umph a-gainst us: de-li-ver us,   O God of Is - ra - el,   out of

SOLO

all   our mi-se-ry and trou - ble.   Un-to thee, O Lord, do I lift up my soul:

FULL

my God, in thee have I trusted, let me not be con-found-ed   Call to re-mem-brance

thy ten-der com-pas-sion   and mer-cy,   O Lord, and thy lo-ving kind-nes-ses

to-wards us, which have been ev-er of old: nei-ther suf-fer our e-ne-mies to

42

8 CALL TO REMEMBRANCE (Cont.)

tri-umph a-gainst us: de -li -ver us,   O God of Is - ra - el, out of all   our

SOLO

mi - se - ry and trou - ble.   Glo -ry be to the Fa-ther, and to the Son, and to the Ho -ly

FULL

Ghost, As it was in the be-gin-ning, is now and ev-er shall be, world with-out end. A - men.

Call to re-mem-brance   thy ten- der com-pas -sion   and mer - cy,   O Lord,   and thy

lov-ing kind-nes-ses to-wards us,   which have been ev-er of   old: nei - ther suf-fer our

e -ne -mies to tri-umph a-gainst us: de -li -ver us, O God of Is - ra - el,   out of

all   our mi - se - ry and trou - ble.

43

9 KYRIE ELEISON

Monastic musicians created melodies for different parts of the Church's calendar to reflect the changing seasons, commemorations, and festivals. The *Kyrie eleison* (the first main movement of the Mass) for the Easter season (known as "Kyrie Lux et Origo"—light and source) has an especially beautiful melody, taking us sometimes to unexpected places. A sweeping melismatic chant such as this takes us to the very heart of the musicianship embodied within the chant repertoire. Sung well, it has energy, freedom, and vitality. You can imagine that monastic musicians would have looked forward to the treat of singing this beautiful music to mark the Easter season.

Do ti la so   So la do la la do do ti so la so fa so so mi
Ky - ri - e _____ e - le - i - son

> This beautiful version of the Kyrie combines a familiar text with longer melismatic phrases. Singers should pay particular attention to the purity of vowels as they sing through the melismas in this plainchant. In the second set of Kyries that begins on the third line, the two notes that come immediately before the jagget note, the "quilisma" (see page 21), should be sung with relatively the same amount of lengthening. The first two notes are emphasized, then move quickly through the jagged note. The purpose of the lengthening is to energize the phrase as it ascends.

TRANSLATION

Lord, have mercy. Lord, have mercy. Lord, have mercy.
Christ, have mercy. Christ, have mercy. Christ, have mercy.
Lord, have mercy. Lord, have mercy. Lord, have mercy.

44

9 KYRIE ELEISON

TRACK 9

211

10 AVE MARIA

The next two chants honor the Blessed Virgin Mary, *Ave Maria* being one of the most famous of all religious texts and one that drew some especially beautiful settings from early Tudor composers such as Robert Parsons and William Byrd. The chant is an example of heightened melismatic writing in which plainchant acquires a rhapsodic quality, especially visible in the words "Maria" and "Dominus." The multiple repeated notes on "Maria"—followed by a return to the high note—have an insistence to them, which is beautiful to sing especially when a true unison is achieved within a group of singers. The chant also shows how interesting rhythmic patterns play their part in plainchant. The music of "Dominus" is a good example of this with its flexible triple note groupings and a duplet at the end of the phrase. This would look quite complicated in modern bar line notation but has a simplicity and clarity about it in original chant notation.

Do ti la so fa Fa so la so la fa la fa so fa mi
A   -   -

The range in this chant is just over an octave and the occurrence of large intervals is frequent compared with most chants (for example, Call to Remembrance or Surrexit Dominus). Negotiating this in one's own voice is perhaps one of the bigger challenges in this piece. Concentration on the direction of the line and awareness of keeping the same space for vowels, especially on descending intervals, will help this tremendously. The familiarity of this text will also come as an advantage to singers while they focus on the musical phrases.

TRANSLATION

Hail Mary, full of grace, the Lord is with you;
Blessed are you among women, and blessed is the fruit of your womb.

46

10 AVE MARIA

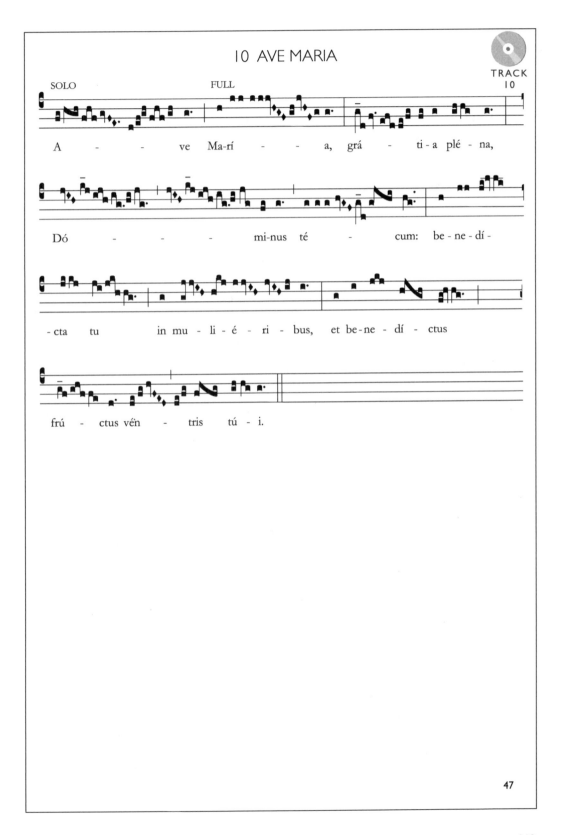

SOLO   FULL

A - - ve Ma-rí - - a, grá - ti-a plé - na,

Dó - - - mi-nus té - cum: be-ne-dí -

- cta tu in mu - li - é - ri - bus, et be-ne - dí - ctus

frú - ctus vén - tris tú - i.

11 SALVE REGINA

There are two settings of the *Salve Regina* in this collection: this florid setting and the simpler setting that appears on page 63. There are four "Anthems to the Blessed Virgin Mary," which are sung liturgically at different times of the year—*Alma Redemptoris Mater, Ave Regina, Regina caeli,* and *Salve Regina*—and each exists in a solemn and a simple tone. The solemn tone—the more florid version—is suitable for more advanced singers, and this can be switched into the Compline liturgy, which concludes this collection, in place of the simple-tone version. Although the chant is less melismatic than the *Ave Maria* on page 47, it is just as florid. The text of the *Salve Regina* has more words than *Ave Maria* so there are fewer instances when a single syllable is sung to an extended phrase. Nevertheless, the singing style learned within *Ave Maria* should be carried over to this chant so the articulation of the words does not slow up the chant or interrupt the florid nature of the piece. It should be sung with grace and reverence. Traditionally, the final three sections, from "O Clemens" are sung at a slower tempo.

There are combinations of notes (compound neums) in "Salve Regina" that you have already seen individually in this book. The complexity of the neums with the Latin text is challenging at first, so it is helpful to learn this chant in smaller sections, gradually adding on sections to what has already been learned. This particular setting uses the flatted seventh scale degree, "ta." Traditionally, the top note of the low-high before the "ta" on the word "nobis" is lengthened. This is perhaps to draw attention to the imploration of the text.

TRANSLATION

Hail, Queen, Mother of mercy; our life, sweetness and hope, hail.

To you we cry, banished children [sons] of Eve.

To you we sigh, groaning and weeping, in this valley of tears.

Quick then, our Advocate, turn your merciful eyes to us.

And show Jesus, blessed fruit of your womb, to us after this exile.

O merciful, O loving, O sweet Virgin Mary.

48

11 SALVE REGINA

SOLO   FULL

Sal - ve, Re - gí - na, má-ter mi-se-ri-cór-di - ae: Ví - ta, dul-cé - do, et spes

nó-stra, sál - ve. Ad te cla-má-mus, éx-su-les fí-li - i Hé - vae. Ad te sus-pi-rá-mus, ge-

mén-tes et flén - tes in hac la-cri-má-rum vál-le. E - ia er-go, Ad-vo-cá - ta nós-tra,

íl-los tú - os mi-se-ri-cór-des ó-cu-los ad nos con-vér - te. Et Jé-sum, be-ne-dí - ctum

frú-ctum vén-tris tú - i, nó - bis post hoc ex-sí-li - um os - tén-de. O clé - mens:

O pí - a: O dúl-cis Vír-go Ma - rí - a.

49

12 ELEGERUNT APOSTOLI STEPHANUM

The final single chant in this collection is much less well known than most of the other chants collected together. It is not often sung, occurring as it does as part of the liturgy for the Feast of St. Stephen. St. Stephen's Day, celebrated on December 26, is often overlooked since it comes the day after Christmas, but its inclusion honors the Oxford college that hosts the Choral Institute at Oxford, St Stephen's House. The buildings of St Stephen's House include two sets of collegiate (inward-facing) wooden singing stalls, which are perfectly designed for the performance of plainchant, so that the two antiphonal choirs for psalm singing (see pages 30 and 35) are set a comfortable distance apart and can hear one another perfectly. Each set of wooden stalls is backed by a curved sound reflector similar to the wooden acoustic panels found on the stage of a modern concert hall so the sound waves do not go only upwards into the lofty vaults but also across to the other side of the choir.

Do ti la so fa mi re do   Do re fa fa mi fa so la mi do re mi so so so so la so
                          E - le - ge   -   -   -   runt_

This chant combines all the elements of the previous pieces in this book. The modality of this chant is unusual to the modern ear. For this reason, the notes are best learned and reinforced using solfège. The melismas should be sung with lots of energy and forward direction to keep the line of the chant moving. When the same note is sung multiple times in a row, the reiterations of the note should be very clear, though not heavy.

TRANSLATION

The Apostles selected Stephen, a deacon, full of faith and the Holy Spirit,

whom the Jews stoned as he prayed and said,

"Lord Jesus, receive my spirit," alleluia.

12 ELEGERUNT APOSTOLI STEPHANUM

SOLO   FULL

E-le-gé - - runt A-pó - sto-li   Sté-pha - num le - ví - tam,

plé - - num fí - - de et Spí - ri - tu Sán-cto: quem

la-pi-da-vé - - runt Ju-daé - i o-rán-tem, et di - cén-tem: Dó - mi - ne

Jé - - su, ác - ci - pe   spí-ri - - tum mé - um, al - le -

- - lú - ia.

51

COMPLINE

Although beautiful plainchant pieces can be used as concert program selections—and can be useful for warm-up or choir study—there is nothing quite like participation in a liturgy for a singer to experience the true feel of plainchant performance. Of all the monastic offices (short services that punctuated the day in monastic life), Compline—the Night Office—is perhaps the most approachable, being short and simple, and being suitable for an atmospheric evening or night-time setting. For a religious community that is used to singing Compline all year round, there are many seasonal variations; but for the sake of clarity I have presented just one of the possible sequences here and have chosen that which would coincide with the summer months (when the Choral Institute at Oxford is held). Those seeking the most authentic versions may prefer to look elsewhere for the whole service in Latin, but the form presented here is that according to the use at St Stephen's House, Oxford, where the service is typically sung in English but with a Latin Anthem at its conclusion. The whole liturgy takes only approximately twenty minutes and proceeds without announcements. Unlike a liturgy such as the Mass, it is not necessary to have a priest present, even for the spoken parts. Compline is a simple sequence of chants that can be sung by a group of lay people.

Many singers who took part in the inaugural Choral Institute who had little religious background—or inclination towards religious practice—were surprised by how easily they took to this simple liturgy and how natural it felt as part of their choral community. Others who came from non-Christian backgrounds felt the same. Those people were able to find that musical, pedagogical, and historical aspects were themselves sufficient to justify participation. With repetition, the familiarity engendered by the sequence became a part of their communal choral experience.

On a more practical level, the presentation of plainchants in this type of uninterrupted sequence shows the importance of each soloist's (cantor's) ability to establish the tonality of a new chant correctly. It does not matter if there is a brief pause before the next item while the soloist works out the pitches for the new chant, and with repetition this will become second nature. If possible, it is better to risk

52

occasional mistakes at first while learning the discipline than to have someone play the intonations on a keyboard, which tends to dull the singer's ability to "feel" the notes and interrupts the purity of the *a cappella* sequence. The pitches of chants do not need to relate to one another in a predetermined way: each intonation of each chant should be chosen to fit the tessitura of the singers present. So provided the relative pitches within each individual item—or small sequence (such as the Responses)—are correct, there is no "right" or "wrong" pitch to choose.

In plainchant notation, the clef is positioned to suit the range of the melody. In this collection, the "Do" clef is always used and is positioned either on the top line or the second line down. In the antiphon to the psalms (page 55), the clef is positioned on the top line. However, immediately following the antiphon, the clef for the psalm (Psalm 4) is on the second line. Do not be alarmed that the clef position changes between those two lines! It is not necessary to take a new pitch between the antiphon and the psalm. The music should continue, as indicated by the guide, which gives you the relationship between the notes in the two lines of music. Because of the clef change, the last note of the antiphon is the same as the first note of the intonation to the psalm.

53

PREPARATION

The officiant knocks his stall. Kneel.

The Lord Almighty grant us a quiet night and a perfect end.
Amen.

Brethren, be sober, be vigilant; because your adversary the devil, as a roaring lion, walketh about, seeking whom he may devour: whom resist, steadfast in the Faith.

But thou, O Lord, have mercy upon us.
Thanks be to God.

Our help is in the name of the Lord.
Who hath made heaven and earth.

After a brief pause for self-examination, the officiant begins the Confiteor:

I confess
to Almighty God and to you, brethren,
that I have sinned exceedingly in thought, word and deed,
through my fault, through my own fault,
through my own most grievous fault.
Wherefore I beg blessed Mary ever-Virgin, all the Angels and Saints,
and you, brethren, to pray for me to the Lord our God.

Almighty God, have mercy upon us, forgive us our sins, and bring us to everlasting life;
Amen.

Stand

PRECES

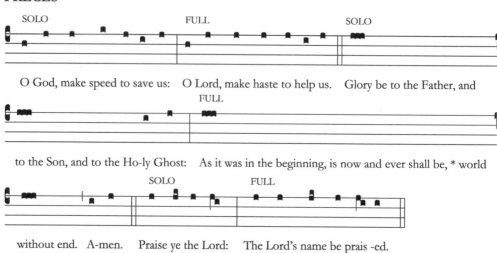

O God, make speed to save us: O Lord, make haste to help us.   Glory be to the Father, and

to the Son, and to the Ho-ly Ghost: As it was in the beginning, is now and ever shall be, * world

without end.   A-men.   Praise ye the Lord: The Lord's name be prais -ed.

54

OFFICE HYMN

SOLO   FULL

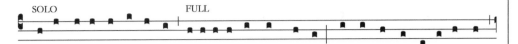

Be-fore the en-ding of the day, Cre-a-tor of the world, we pray That with un-won-ted fa-vor thou

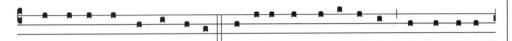

Wouldst be our Guard and Keep-er now. From all ill dreams de-fend our eyes, From night-ly fears

and fan-ta-sies; Tread un-der foot our ghost-ly foe, That no pol-lu-tion we may know. O Fa-ther,

that we ask be done, Through Je-sus Christ, thine on-ly Son; Who, with the Ho-ly Ghost and thee,

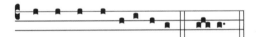

Doth live and reign e-ter-nal-ly.   A-men.

Sit

ANTIPHON TO THE PSALMS,
PSALM 4 AND PSALM 31 (1-6)

SOLO   FULL

Have mer-cy   up-on me, O God,   and heark-en un-to my prayer.

SOLO (from CHOIR 1)   CHOIR 1

1. Hear me when I call O God, * defender of my right: thou didst free me when I was hard pressed, *

CHOIR 2

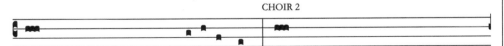

have mercy upon me and hearken un-to my prayer. 2. O ye sons of men, * how long shall my glory be

CHOIR 1

re-viled: how long will ye have such pleasure in folly and seek af -ter false-hood? 3. Know this also, *

that the Lord hath chosen to himself the man that is god-ly: when I call upon the Lord he will hear

CHOIR 2

me. 4. Stand in awe and sin not: commune with your own heart within your cham-ber and be still.

CHOIR 1   CHOIR 2

5. Offer sacrifices in their appointed sea-sons: and put your trust in the Lord. 6. There be many

that say * 'Who will show us any good?' Lord lift thou up the light of thy coun-ten-ance up-on us.

CHOIR 1

7. Thou hast put gladness in my heart: more than men have when their corn and wine in-crease.

CHOIR 2

8. I will lay me down in peace and take my rest: for it is thou Lord only that makest me dwell in

CHOIR 1   CHOIR 2

safe-ty. Glory be to the Father, and to the Son: and to the Ho-ly Ghost; As it was in the beginning, *

is now, and ever shall be: world with-out end. A-men.

SOLO (from CHOIR 1)   CHOIR 1

1. In thee O Lord have I put my trust: let me never be put to confusion, * deliver me in thy

CHOIR 2   CHOIR 1

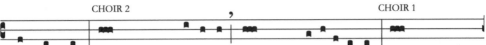

right-eous-ness 2. Bow down thine ear to me: O haste thee to de-li-ver me. 3. And be thou my

CHOIR 2

strong rock and house of de-fence: that thou may-est save me. 4. For thou art my strong rock and

CHOIR 1

my cast-le: be thou also my guide, * and lead me for thy name's sake. 5. Draw me out of the net that

CHOIR 2

they have laid privily for me: for thou art my strength. 6. Into thy hands I commend my spi -rit:

CHOIR 1

for thou hast redeemed me, O Lord thou God of truth.   Glory be to the Father, and to the Son:

CHOIR 2

and to the Ho-ly Ghost; As it was in the beginning, * is now, and ever shall be: world with-out

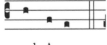

end. A-men.

57

Have mer-cy   up-on me, O God,   and heark-en un-to my prayer.

SCRIPTURE READING
MATTHEW 11. 28-30

Come unto me, all ye that labour and are heavy laden, and I will give you rest.
Take my yoke upon you, and learn of me; for I am meek and lowly in heart:
and ye shall find rest unto your souls. For my yoke is easy, and my burden is light.

Thanks be to God.

A brief period of silence follows the reading.

RESPONSORY

In-to thy hands, O Lord,   I com-mend my spi-rit.

In-to thy hands, O Lord,   I com-mend my spi-rit.

For thou hast re-deem-ed me,   O Lord thou God of truth.

I com-mend my spi-rit.

58

SOLO

Glory be to the Father, and to the Son,   and to the Ho-ly Ghost.

FULL

In-to thy hands, O Lord,   I com-mend my spi-rit.

SOLO

Keep me, O Lord, as the apple of an eye.

FULL

Hide me under the shadow of thy wings.

Stand

GOSPEL CANTICLE AND ANTIPHON

SOLO   FULL

Pre-serve us,   O Lord, while wak-ing   and guard us while sleep-ing, that a-wake we may

watch with Christ, and a-sleep we may rest in peace.

59

SOLO (from CHOIR 1) CHOIR 1 CHOIR 2

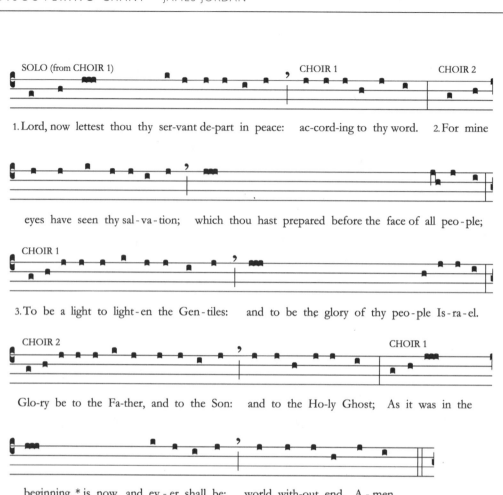

1. Lord, now lettest thou thy ser-vant de-part in peace: ac-cord-ing to thy word.   2. For mine

eyes have seen thy sal-va-tion;   which thou hast prepared before the face of all peo-ple;

CHOIR 1

3. To be a light to light-en the Gen-tiles: and to be the glory of thy peo-ple Is-ra-el.

CHOIR 2 CHOIR 1

Glo-ry be to the Fa-ther, and to the Son: and to the Ho-ly Ghost; As it was in the

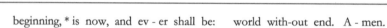

beginning, * is now, and ev-er shall be: world with-out end. A-men.

FULL

Pre-serve us, O Lord, while wak-ing and guard us while sleep-ing, that a-wake we may

watch with Christ, and a-sleep we may rest in peace.

Kneel

SUFFRAGES

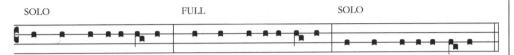

Lord, have mer-cy up-on us.   Christ, have mer-cy up-on us.   Lord, have mer-cy up-on us.

Our Father,
who art in heaven, hallowed be thy name; thy kingdom come; thy will be done,
on earth as it is in heaven. Give us this day our daily bread;
and forgive us our trespasses,
as we forgive them that trespass against us;
and lead us not into temptation, but deliver us from evil. Amen.

Blessed art thou, Lord God of our fa-thers: To be praised and glorified above all for ev-er.

Let us bless the Father, the Son, and the Ho-ly Ghost: Let us praise him and magnify him for ev-er.

Blessed art thou, O Lord, in the firmament of hea-ven: To be praised and glorified above all

for ev-er.   The almighty and most merciful Lord guard us and give us his bles-sing.   A-men.

Wilt thou not turn again and quick-en us: That thy people may rejoice in thee?

O Lord, show thy mercy up-on us: And grant us thy sal-va-tion.

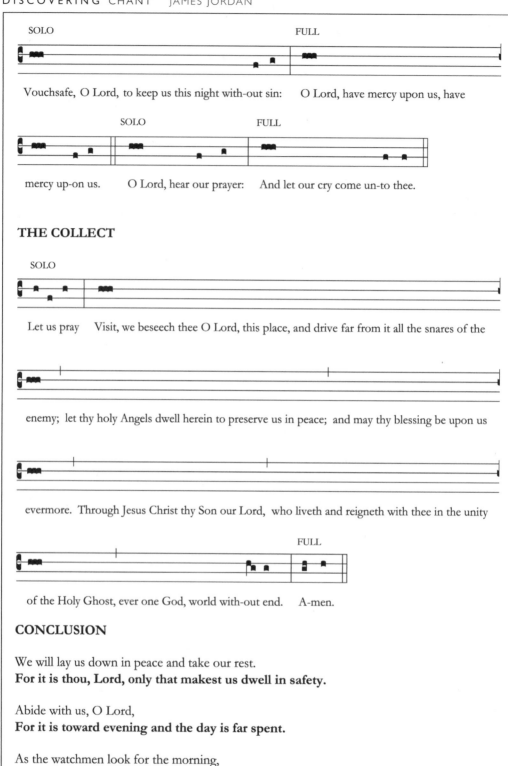

SOLO   FULL

Vouchsafe, O Lord, to keep us this night with-out sin: O Lord, have mercy upon us, have

SOLO   FULL

mercy up-on us.   O Lord, hear our prayer: And let our cry come un-to thee.

THE COLLECT

SOLO

Let us pray   Visit, we beseech thee O Lord, this place, and drive far from it all the snares of the

enemy; let thy holy Angels dwell herein to preserve us in peace; and may thy blessing be upon us

evermore. Through Jesus Christ thy Son our Lord, who liveth and reigneth with thee in the unity

FULL

of the Holy Ghost, ever one God, world with-out end.   A-men.

CONCLUSION

We will lay us down in peace and take our rest.
For it is thou, Lord, only that makest us dwell in safety.

Abide with us, O Lord,
For it is toward evening and the day is far spent.

As the watchmen look for the morning,
So do we look for thee, O Christ.

Come with the dawning of the day,
And make thyself known in the breaking of bread.

SOLO   FULL   SOLO   FULL

O Lord, hear our prayer: And let our cry come un-to thee. Let us bless the Lord: Thanks be to

SOLO

God. The Almighty and merciful Lord, the Father, the Son, and the Holy Ghost, vouchsafe to

FULL

bless us and pre-serve us. A-men.

Stand. We turn and face the statue of Our Lady.

SOLO   FULL

Sal-ve, Re-gí-na, má-ter mi-se-ri-cór-di-ae: Ví-ta, dul-cé-do, et spes nós-tra, sál-ve. Ad te

cla-má-mus, éx-su-les, fí-li-i Hé-vae. Ad te sus-pi-rá-mus, ge-mén-tes et flén-tes in hac lac-ri-

má-rum vál-le. E-ia er-go, Ad-vo-cá-ta nós-tra, íl-los tú-os mi-se-ri-cór-des ó-cu-los ad nos

con-vér-te. Et Jé-sum, be-ne-dí-ctum frú-ctum vén-tris tú-i, nó-bis post hoc ex-sí-li-um

os-tén-de. O clé-mens: O pí-a: O dúl-cis Vír-go Ma-rí-a.

63

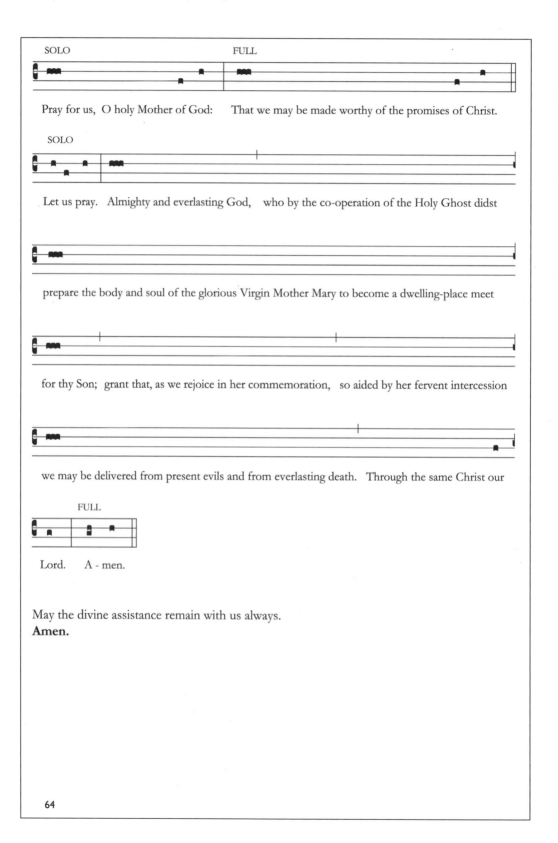

SOLO   FULL

Pray for us, O holy Mother of God: That we may be made worthy of the promises of Christ.

SOLO

Let us pray. Almighty and everlasting God,   who by the co-operation of the Holy Ghost didst

prepare the body and soul of the glorious Virgin Mother Mary to become a dwelling-place meet

for thy Son; grant that, as we rejoice in her commemoration,   so aided by her fervent intercession

we may be delivered from present evils and from everlasting death.   Through the same Christ our

FULL

Lord.   A - men.

May the divine assistance remain with us always.
Amen.

64

ABOUT THE
CHORAL MUSIC INSTITUTE
AT OXFORD

The Choral Music Institute at Oxford, a partnership between Westminster Choir College of Rider University and St Stephen's House, a permanent Hall of Oxford, was established in 2013. Co-directors James Whitbourn, a research fellow at St Stephen's House, and James Jordan, professor and senior conductor at Westminster Choir College, envisioned this program to provide academic experiences unique to Oxford, offering conductors a chance to experience study and artistry through human connection at the highest levels. The intensive curriculum provides a deeply immersive experience that has at its core the GRAMMY-nominated Westminster Williamson Voices in residence at the Institute.

The Choral Institute at Oxford is housed within St Stephen's House at Oxford, an architectural masterpiece designed by renowned Anglican architect G. F. Bodley, architect of the National Cathedral. Each summer, the Institute mounts a rigorous professional program of study and performance that culminates in each of the conductors conducting a performance of the studied work. Score analysis, conducting study, and diverse ancillary lectures pertaining to aspects of music education, sacred music, musicology, performance practices, and musical style comprise the curriculum each summer. The curricular offerings are different each summer so as to allow for the continued and ongoing growth of conductors who choose to return for study each summer.

The Institute is open to both conducting participants and non-conducting auditors by application and acceptance by the directors. The Institute welcomes all levels of conductors. Further information about the program can be found along with enrollment information at www.rider.edu/Oxford.

ABOUT THE AUTHORS

JAMES JORDAN

GRAMMY-nominated conductor James Jordan is recognized and praised around the musical world as one of the nation's pre-eminent conductors, writers, and innovators in choral music. A master teacher, researcher, and scholar, Dr. Jordan's pioneering writing and research concerning the use of Laban Effort-Shape for the teaching of conducting and movement to children and adults has dramatically changed teaching in both of those disciplines. Called the "Father of the Case Study," he was the first researcher to bring forward the idea of the case study as a viable and valuable form of research for the training and education of teachers.

Dr. Jordan has had the privilege of studying under the most-renowned conductors and teachers of the past fifty years, including Elaine Brown, Wilhelm Ehmann, Frauke Haasemann, Volker Hempfling, and Edwin Gordon. His books and pedagogical materials have provided new teaching directions in group vocal technique, rhythm pedagogy, skill building within the choral ensemble using aural immersion solfege, conducting and conducting pedagogy, and rehearsal technique. His six books, beginning with *The Musician's Soul* and continuing with *The Musician's Spirit, The Musician's Walk, Toward Center, The Musician's Breath,* and *The Musician's Trust,* explore in depth the human aspects of music making. He has also collaborated on *Lighting a Candle,* a book of writings by his teacher, Elaine Brown, who helped form his lifelong philosophical foundation for his books.

Dr. Jordan is the most-published performer/author in the world: he has authored more than 35 books on all aspects of the choral art and has been described as a "visionary" by *Choral Journal. Gramophone* hailed him as a conductor of "forceful and intimate choral artistry." *American Record Guide* has praised his recordings as being "without peer." His career and publications have been devoted to innovative educational changes in the choral art, which have been embraced around the world. His book *Evoking Sound* was named as a "must read" on a list of six books by *Choral Journal.*

At Westminster Choir College, Dr. Jordan is Professor of Conducting and Senior Conductor, and he conducts the Westminster Schola Cantorum and the internationally acclaimed Westminster Williamson Voices. Praised on both sides of the Atlantic, the Westminster Williamson Voices has become one of the leading choral ensembles in the world for the performance of music of our time. This book is an outgrowth of the unique pedagogies that Dr. Jordan has developed for use in rehearsal by the Williamson Voices, making the group one of the leading "living choral laboratories" in the world. Accolades for the choir from composers praise the ensemble for its sound and human connection.

James Jordan and the Westminster Williamson Voices have made two critically acclaimed recordings of the music of James Whitbourn on the Naxos label. *Living Voices* was described as "superb" by *Gramophone.* And *Annelies,* the first major choral setting of *The Diary of Anne Frank* (2013 GRAMMY-nominated recording for Best Choral Performance), was hailed by *BBC Music Magazine* for its "poignant intertwining of voices and instruments." Regarding *Annelies, Gramophone* wrote, "Jordan's instinctive understanding of the score makes this a profound and emotionally charged experience."

Dr. Jordan also serves as Executive Editor of the *Evoking Sound Choral Series* (including the *Music from Westminster* and *Music for Young Voices* series), published by GIA Publications in Chicago. This series, now with over 150 published works, presents choral literature at graded levels for middle school, high school, and college choirs. In addition to new compositions by America's finest composers, the series also presents new editions of standard choral repertoire, edited with singers in mind. Also unique to this series are solfege editions that utilize Jordan's groundbreaking approach to the use of solfege in choral ensembles, with accurate aural analysis as the basis of this approach.

Dr. Jordan's residencies, master classes, and guest conducting have taken him throughout the United States, Canada, Europe, and Australia He has conducted more than 30 All-State Choirs. He has been named to the choral panel for The National Endowment for the Arts and to the Temple University Gallery of Success, and was awarded an honorary Doctor of Music by the University of Aberdeen in Scotland in recognition for his contributions to choral music around the world.

Additionally, Dr. Jordan directs two of the leading programs in the world for the lifelong education of conductors. For the past 15 years, thousands of conductors have journeyed to the Westminster campus, and most recently to Oxford, to enrich their conducting understandings and themselves. He serves as artistic director of the Westminster Conducting Institute, one of the nation's leading summer programs for the training and education of conductors, and as co-director (with James Whitbourn) of the newly established (2013) Choral Institute at Oxford, which is a unique partnership with St Stephen's House, a permanent private hall of the University of Oxford (www.rider.edu/Oxford).

JAMES WHITBOURN

James Whitbourn is a GRAMMY-nominated composer recognized by *The Observer* as "a truly original communicator in modern British choral music." A graduate of Magdalen College, University of Oxford, his career in music began in the BBC, for whom he has worked as composer, conductor, producer, and presenter. His compositional output is admired for its direct connection with performers and audiences worldwide and for its ability to "expand the experience of classical music beyond the edges of the traditional map of classical styles" (Tom Manoff, NPR).

Whitbourn's largest composition is the concert-length choral work *Annelies*, the first major choral setting of *The Diary of Anne Frank*. Other notable works include *Luminosity*, written for Westminster Choir College and the ArcheDream Dance Ensemble, and the *Son of God Mass* for saxophone, choir, and organ. His varied output includes several works written with and for his friend, the late Robert Tear, and works commissioned for the enthronement of the Bishop of Salisbury, an Easter Day Festival at King's College Cambridge, and the 1400th anniversary of Rochester Cathedral. He has also collaborated with former Poet Laureate Andrew Motion, Michael Symmons Roberts, and Desmond Tutu.

Whitbourn's choral works have been performed in many prestigious venues and are present on acclaimed recordings, including four complete discs of his choral music. Of the latest of these—*Annelies* (Naxos)—*Gramophone* writes "the greatest accomplishment here is that James Whitbourn has written some music of great beauty," with *Choir and Organ* adding, "Whitbourn's devastatingly beautiful and restrained treatment of the subject matter makes it all the more poignant." His first Naxos recording, *Luminosity*, reached No. 3 on Classical Billboard, and of the "stunning music" heard on *Living Voices*, *Choral Journal* promised that listeners "will be transformed by the sheer beauty of the sonic experience."

The greater part of Whitbourn's compositional output is in vocal and choral music, but his range of style incorporates the lush symphonic scoring heard in his early BBC landmark series *Son of God* (whose seminal themes form his best-known work, *Son of God Mass* for choir, saxophone, and organ) and the inventive orchestral textures of *Annelies*. His orchestral commissions include the award-winning work *Pika*, based on the bombing of Hiroshima, one of three large-scale compositions for symphony orchestra written with poet Michael Symmons Roberts and performed by the BBC Philharmonic, who have also recorded many of his television scores.

Annelies, a concert-length work for soprano soloist, choir, and ensemble, exists in two scorings, the larger of which (for symphony orchestra) was premiered by Leonard Slatkin at London's Cadogan Hall in 2005. The work went on to receive its U.S. premiere in 2007 and was premiered in a new chamber version by violinist Daniel Hope and American soprano Arianna Zukerman at The Hague, Netherlands, on Anne Frank's 80th birthday in 2009. Its libretto is drawn from *The Diary of Anne Frank,* crafted into a new translation by Melanie Challenger.

Whitbourn's choral works have been performed on every inhabited continent of the world, especially in North America and mainland Europe. He enjoys a close relationship with Westminster Choir College in Princeton, New Jersey, where his music is often performed and where he has served as Composer-in-Residence. He also has a special relationship with the Choir of King's College, Cambridge, with whom he has worked for more than twenty years and for whom he composed *Magnificat and Nunc Dimittis collegium regale,* premiered on Easter Day in 2005. Whitbourn has been commissioned to compose the music to mark several national and international events, including the BBC's title music for the funeral of Queen Elizabeth, the Queen Mother, and music for the national commemoration of 9/11 at Westminster Abbey (subsequently performed in New York on the first anniversary of the attacks). He also composed music for the BBC coverage of the 60th anniversary of D-Day.

Many of Whitbourn's choral works have been recorded by the Choir of Clare College, Cambridge, with saxophonist John Harle and tenor Robert Tear under Timothy Brown (Et Cetera KTC 1248), *Commotio,* with violist Levine Andrade and tenor Christopher Gillett, conducted by Matthew Berry (Naxos 8.572103), and The Westminster Williamson Voices, conducted by James Jordan (Naxos 8.572737). The Westmintser Williamson Voices' Naxos recording of *Annelies* under James Jordan was nominated for a GRAMMY Award for Best Choral Performance in 2014.

James Whitbourn is popular on both sides of the Atlantic as a choral advisor, and he also enjoys a profile as a conductor and producer, having received three

GRAMMY nominations along with many other international awards and nominations. He is a regular participant in choral preparation workshops and has worked with students at Princeton University, Rider University, Oxford University, Cambridge University, and other educational and choral establishments. In addition to conducting the BBC Philharmonic, the Academy of St. Martin in the Fields, and other leading orchestras, he directs the London-based vocal ensemble, The Choir, whose acclaimed DVD recording of John Tavener's choral music received a *Gramophone* nomination.

James Whitbourn is an Honorary Research Fellow of St Stephen's House, Oxford, one of Oxford University's six permanent private halls. He is also a visiting lecturer at Royal Holloway, University of London. Since 2001, he has held an exclusive publishing agreement with Chester Music, London.

ISABELLA BURNS

Isabella Burns grew up in Northern California, where her family attended a Latin Mass parish. This began her early and constant exposure to plainchant and sacred music. At the age of eight, she became a chorister at St. Stephen the First Martyr Roman Catholic Church in Sacramento, California. While there, she sang and studied under the direction of Jeffrey Morse, long-time student of Dr. Mary Berry. She remained a chorister there for ten years until she finished high school. During that time, in addition to two weekly rehearsals the choristers at St. Stephen's became proficient in chant while singing for multiple services and feast days, sometimes as many as six per week.

Burns currently studies at Westminster Choir College, where she is pursuing a degree in Sacred Music. A member of the GRAMMY-nominated Westminster Williamson Voices, where she serves as a section leader, she collaborated with James Jordan in teaching and developing pedagogical procedures to teach the Williamson Voices to sing plainchant. She continues to sing chant for the Latin Mass at St. John's Roman Catholic Church in Allentown, New Jersey, while studying in Princeton.

DOMINIC GREGORIO

Dominic Gregorio is Director of Choral Music and Assistant Professor of Choral Music at the University of Regina. He holds a Doctor of Musical Arts from the University of Southern California, writing the first doctoral dissertation on the choral music of Tarik O'Regan (b. 1978). His interests include new movements in choral music, interdisciplinary performance, and exploring the broad spectrum of vocal ensemble music. As a baritone, he is interested in German lied and French chanson performance, and undertook specialized training at the Vienna University of Music. Trained in Rishikesh, India, the birthplace of yoga, Dr. Gregorio teaches yoga for musicians and is interested in the benefits of yoga, meditation, and breathing exercises for singers.

Dr. Gregorio is a former conductor of the McMaster University Choir, Gay Men's Chorus of Los Angeles, USC Thornton Opera, USC Thornton Apollo Men's Choir, Toronto Singing Out, Siren – The University of Guelph Women's Choir, and a former assistant conductor of the Guelph Youth Singers, USC Thornton Chamber Singers, Taipei Philharmonic Foundation (台北愛樂), and the University of Guelph Symphonic Choir.

STEVEN PILKINGTON

Steven Pilkington is an outstanding educator and producer of sacred music in the American Protestant tradition. An associate professor at Westminster Choir College, Dr. Pilkington has taught every aspect of the church music curriculum for over twenty years. His teaching is known for its breadth, depth, and creative attention to the complexities of making music in the postmodern American church. As an active church musician, he has served as director of music and organist at Christ Church, United Methodist at 60th and Park in the heart of New York City for nearly two decades. During his tenure there, he has built a fully graded choral and handbell program crowned by an exceptional mixed choir of volunteers and professionals who sing a rich variety of sacred literature ranging from gospel to chant and contemporary commissions to works from the classical canon. Many of his organ scholars have gone on to leading positions in some of America's finest churches, including Harvard Chapel, Fifth Avenue Presbyterian, and Riverside Church. Additionally, Dr. Pilkington is a published author and composer of organ and liturgical music.

BIBLIOGRAPHY

Apel, Willi. *Gregorian Chant*. Bloomington: Indiana University Press, 1990.

Berry, Mary. *Cantors: A Collection of Gregorian Chant*s. Cambridge: Cambridge University Press, 1979.

———. *Plainchant for Everyone*. Surrey: The Royal School of Church Music, 1979.

Cain, Susan. *Quiet*. New York: Crown Publishers, 2012.

Cooke, Philip, and David Maw. *The Music of Herbert Howells*. Woodbridge, Suffolk: The Boydell Press, 2013.

Crocker, Richard L. *An Introduction to Gregorian Chant*. New Haven, CT: Yale University Press, 2000.

Custer, Gerald and Henson, Blake. *From Words to Music: User's Guide to Text for Choral Musicians*. Chicago: GIA, 2014

Dowrick, Stephanie. *Intimacy and Solitude*. New York: W.W. Norton and Company, 1991.

Ehmann, Wilhelm. *Choral Directing*. Minneapolis, MN: Augsburg, 1968.

Gajard, Dom Joseph. *The Rhythm of Plainsong*. Richmond, VA: The Church Music Association of America, 2007.

———. *The Solesmes Method*. Collegeville, MN: The Liturgical Press, 1960.

Goleman, Daniel. *Focus*. New York: HarperCollins, 2013.

Goodchild, Mary Antione. *Gregorian Chant*. New York: Ginn and Co., 1944.

Gordon, Edwin E. *Learning Sequences in Music*. Chicago: GIA Publications, 2012.

———. *The Aural/ Visual Experience of Music Literacy*. Chicago: GIA Publications, 2004.

Herbert, Rembert. *Entrances: Gregorian Chant in Daily Life*. New York: Church Publishing Inc., 1999.

Hiley, David. *Cambridge Introductions to Music: Gregorian Chant*. Cambridge: Cambridge University Press, 2009.

Hourlier, Dom Jacques. *Reflections on the Spirituality of Gregorian Chant*. Brewster, MA: Paraclete Press, 2012.

———. *Reflections on the Spirituality of Gregorian Chant*. New edition revised, expanded and translated by Dom Gregory Casprini and Robert Edmonson. Brewster, MA: Paraclete Press, 1995.

Inchausti, Robert. *Thinking through Thomas Merton*. Albany, NY: State University of New York Press, 2014.

Jones, Noel. *A Beginner's Guide to Reading Gregorian Chant Notation*. Englewood, TN: Frog Music Press.

Jordan, James, Sonya Garfinkle, and Janet Yamron. *Lighting a Candle: The Writings and Wisdom of Elaine Brown*. Chicago: GIA Publications, 2014.

Jung, C. G. *Synchronicity: An Acausal Connecting Principle*. Princeton, NJ: Princeton University Press, 1960.

Kierkegaard, Soren. *Purity of Heart Is to Will One Thing*. Lexington, KY: Feather Trail Press, 2009.

———. *Works of Love*. New York: HarperPerennial, 2009.

Kramer, Lawrence. *Expression and Truth*. Berkeley: University of California Press, 2012.

Le Mee, Katherine. *The Benedictine Gift to Music*. Mahwah, NJ: Paulist Press, 2003.

Lewis, C. S. *Essay Collection*. New York: HarperCollins, 2000.

Lewis, Sarah. *The Rise: Creativity, the Gift of Failure, and the Search for Mastery*. New York: Simon and Schuster, 2014.

Lowinsky, Edward. *Tonality and Atonality in Sixteenth Century Music*. Berkeley: University of California Press, 1962.

Mandela, Nelson. *Conversations with Myself*. New York: Farrar, Strauss, and Giroux, 2010.

McGinnis, Mark W. *The Wisdom of the Benedictine Elders*. New York: BlueBridge, 2005.

Moore, Thomas. *A Religion of One's Own*. New York: Gotham Books, 2014.

———. *Care of the Soul*. London: Piatkus Books, 2012.

Nouwen, Henri J. M. *The Way of the Heart*. New York: Ballantine Books, 1981.

O'Donohue, John. *Beauty: The Invisible Embrace*. New York: HarperCollins Publishers, 2004.

Parker, Alice. *The Anatomy of Melody*. Chicago: GIA Publications, 2006.

———. *The Answering Voice*. Chicago: GIA Publications, 2014.

Restagno, Enzo, Leopold Brauneiss, and Saale Kareda. *Arvo Part in Conversation*. London: Dalkey Archive Press, 2012.

Rilke, Rainer Maria. *Poems from the Book of Hours*. New York: New Directions Books, 2009.

Rohr, Richard. *Immortal Diamond*. San Francisco: Jossey-Bass, 2013.

———. *Simplicity: The Freedom of Letting Go*. New York: The Crossroads Publishing Company, 1991.

Sauliner, Dom Daniel. Mary Berry, trans. *Gregorian Chant: A Guide to History and Liturgy*. Brewster, MA: Paraclete Press, 2010.

Stapert, Calvin R. *A New Song for an Old World: Musical Thought in the Early Church*. Grand Rapids, MI: William B. Eerdmans, 2007.

Steindl-Rast, David, and Sharon Lebell. *Music of Silence*. Berkeley, CA: Ulysses Press, 2002.

Storch, Laila. *Marcel Tabuteau*. Bloomington: Indiana University Press, 2008.

Taruskin, Richard. *The Oxford History of Western Music, Vol. 1: The Earliest Notations to the Sixteenth Century*. Oxford: Oxford University Press, 2005.

Thurmond, James Morgan. *Note Grouping: A Method for Achieving Expression and Style in Musical Performance*. Camp Hill, PA: JMT Publications, 1982.

Turner, Edith. *Communitas*. Kindle edition. New York: Palgrave Macmillan, 2012.